William Augustus Edmond Ussher

The post-Tertiary Geology of Cornwall

William Augustus Edmond Ussher

The post-Tertiary Geology of Cornwall

ISBN/EAN: 9783337091798

Printed in Europe, USA, Canada, Australia, Japan

Cover: Foto ©ninafisch / pixelio.de

More available books at **www.hansebooks.com**

THE

POST-TERTIARY GEOLOGY

OF

CORNWALL.

BY

W. A. E. USSHER, F.G.S.,

OF H.M. GEOLOGICAL SURVEY OF ENGLAND AND WALES.

1879.

PRINTED FOR PRIVATE CIRCULATION,

BY STEPHEN AUSTIN AND SONS, HERTFORD.

CONTENTS.

PREFATORY STATEMENT   1

PART I.—THE PLEISTOCENE DEPOSITS OF CORNWALL   9

PART II.—A CLASSIFICATION OF THE PLEISTOCENE DEPOSITS OF

     CORNWALL   37

TABLE OF CLASSIFICATION   50

NOTES ON THE PLEISTOCENE DEPOSITS OF THE CORNISH COAST NEAR

     PADSTOW   53

CORNISH POST-TERTIARY GEOLOGY.

PREFATORY STATEMENT.

In the course of a series of articles on the recent geology of Cornwall, begun in January last, in the "Geological Magazine," I referred in the March number, p. 102, to papers on the same subject which I had submitted to the Geological Society. These papers contain the bulk of original observations made by me during leaves of absence in 1876, and also embody such quotations as are necessary to establish the classification put forward, being the records of phenomena which could in no way come under my personal observation. The articles in the "Geological Magazine" were intended to supplement this general work of description and classification, by bringing out the historical part of the subject, the mass of bibliography, and detailed accounts of each section of the paper: so that the combined papers might bring into one view all that had previously been written on the subject, and show that the reasoning was logically founded on fact, and that facts not coming within the author's direct observation had not been distorted to accord with his views. The whole subject was originally embodied in a single paper too voluminous to obtain admission in any Society's Journal. It lay dormant for two years, during which I neglected no opportunity of adding to the details which a survey of the superficial deposits of Devon and Somerset, extending over the six previous years, had enabled me to accumulate. The general results of my survey of the recent deposits of Devon and Cornwall are to be

1

found in a paper, entitled "The Chronological Value of the Pleis-tocene Deposits of Devon," Quart. Journ. Geol. Soc., 1878, vol. xxxiv. pp. 449-458. Finding the results arrived at by independent studies of Devon and Cornwall dovetail, I felt bound to bring out my views respecting the latter county, and accordingly recon-structed the original MSS., giving the general results in the papers here prefaced, viz. a General Description (Part I.) and Classification (Part II.), and a separate account of the most in-teresting combination of recent geological phenomena anywhere to be found on the south-western coasts of England.

In transmitting these papers to the Geological Society, in October, 1878, I stipulated that in the event of any abridgment being decided on by the Council, the MSS. should be returned to me, and no abstracts printed in the Journal. On December 4th, 1878, brief abstracts of the papers were read, in my unavoidable absence; and, considering the nature of the subject, I do not think better abstracts could have been made, as far as one can judge from the *resumés* in the fortnightly "Abstracts of Proceedings." On February 19th, 1879, I received the following letter:

Geological Society, Burlington House, W.

MY DEAR MR. USSHER,—The resolution passed by the Council was to the effect that your two papers on Cornish Pleistocene Geology should be printed "in short abstract in accordance with the opinion of the Referee." The opinions expressed by the Referee I have copied, and now inclose.— Yours truly,

W. S. DALLAS.

The form for the guidance of the Referee is as follows :—

1st. Is it desirable that the paper, as it stands, should be published in the Quarterly Journal of the Society, as containing new facts, or new views of the bearing of admitted facts, or appa-rently well-founded corrections of important errors as to matters of fact, published in the Journal of the Society or elsewhere? or,

2nd. Is it desirable that any part of the paper should be omitted, as merely general observations, or as unnecessarily controversial, or as containing expressions liable to give just cause of offence, by reason of their personality, or otherwise? or,

3rd. Can the Paper, for other reasons, be altered or abridged, without detriment, either in the text or in the illustrations? if so, you will please to mark, in pencil, the parts which, in your opinion, may be so altered or abridged; or,

4th. Would an abstract, only, give all that is important in the paper? and would such abstract require any woodcut or other illustration, regard being had to previous publications on the same class of subjects?

5th. If any illustrations accompany the paper, can any one, or more, or all of them be dispensed with, being of a kind either well known, or merely ideal, or too indefinite, or incorrect?

The following is the opinion of the Referee:—

The Pleistocene History of Cornwall. Part I.

(1). "This paper does not comply with any of the requirements under the first query (see form herewith inclosed). The avowed object of the communication was not to record any original personal observations, but to arrange the plentiful material of Messrs. Boase, Carne, Henwood, and others, in a connected history of the Pleistocene period in Cornwall, an attempt not hitherto made.

"The author was in Cornwall in 1876, and visited certain localities, of which sections and descriptions had already been given in well-known publications. Such being the nature of the paper, it cannot be recommended for publication in the Quarterly Journal, in accordance with first query.

(4). "An abstract would suffice."

Pleistocene History of Cornwall. Part II.

"A classification of the Pleistocene deposits of Cornwall. The author's method of treating this part of his subject leads to a great deal of repetition of Part I. There are not any new views to warrant the publication, in extenso, of such a memoir in the Journal. I would point out the age assigned to the oldest deposits, Crousa Downs, etc., etc., which is just that which Sir H. de la Beche speculated upon.

"So also the 'Classification' is merely the order of sequence for the rest of the series, which that geologist has adopted in his report."

PLEISTOCENE NOTES ON THE COAST OF CORNWALL, NEAR PADSTOW.

"This locality was visited and described by Mr. Henwood in 1858. The several phenomena of blown sands, either loose or cemented, with littoral and sand-hill shells, with an under-layer of old vegetable surface, all occur there, but not with so distinct relations as at so many other places on the Western Coasts.

"In the greater portion of the paper the author argues out certain hypothetical considerations, which, however, do not conduce to any very definite views. In this communication, as in the two former, the term Pleistocene has been adopted, but there is no definite explanation as to the precise portion of geological time which is thereby meant.

"Abstracts of these communications will suffice."

Such is the substance of the Referee's report.

Having called attention to the state of the Referee system at the Anniversary Meeting of the Society, on February 21st, I sent in the following reply to Mr. Dallas's letter of the 19th :—

DEAR SIR,—I have to acknowledge the receipt of the decision of the Council respecting certain papers of mine on the Pleistocene Geology of Cornwall. In transmitting the papers in question to you, I signified my desire that the MSS. should be returned, and no abstract, however brief, printed in the Quarterly Journal, in the event of the least abstraction being decided on by the Council, except in the matter of illustrations, of which some were marked as capable of being dispensed with. I now ask that this request should be complied with, unless the Council decide that the papers in question be printed in full, after consideration of the accompanying memoranda, embodying my objections to the decision of the Referee.—I am, Sir, yours faithfully,   W. A. E. USSHER.

The following answer to the Referee was accompanied by the original notes made by me in Cornwall on maps and in note book, to vindicate the title of the paper to originality in substance as well as in form.

ANSWERS TO THE REFEREE'S REPORT ON PAPERS RELATING TO THE
PLEISTOCENE HISTORY OF CORNWALL.

In answer to the first objection, I have to adduce the Referee's quotation of the words, "in a connected history of the Pleistocene

Period in Cornwall;" *such a history* having *never* before been attempted, it was absolutely necessary to collect the scattered, and often casual, observations of previous workers, more especially those relating to submerged forests and stream-tin sections, which I could have no opportunities of observing; but the major part of these quotations were reserved for separate publication, such only as were considered indispensable to illustrate the inferences drawn, and for purposes of classification, being retained in the papers under consideration.

As to original observations, I can only submit to the Council the maps on which my observations were made and the notes written on the spot. These will establish my claim to have exceeded all previous observers in amount of *original* observation respecting the Post-Tertiary Geology of Cornwall. The Referee states that the localities visited by me had previously been described with sections. Many localities had been described, and a few sections had been given; but the descriptions were wanting *in essential particulars*, and the sections mere sketches. In almost all of them *the Head* was barely mentioned, whereas in my paper it has been assigned *an important place*; De la Beche neglected it, and Mr. Godwin-Austen gave very few observations of its occurrence in Cornwall, and applied solutions to account for it, which I consider inadmissible in some cases. Even if, in other respects, my paper were a replica of De la Beche's GENERAL OBSERVATIONS on the recent geology of Cornwall, *the descriptions of this stony loam, or Head, and its insertion in the sequence of deposits, would redeem the paper from every objection brought against it by the Referee.*

The repetition complained of in Part II. was occasioned by the construction of the paper to permit of division into separate parts both in reading and printing, if necessary.

Notwithstanding this alleged repetition, I have been accused of adopting De la Beche's views, whereas in the essential particulars of the relative age of the Submerged Forests and *Raised Beaches, a reference to p.* 425, *lines* 20, *etc., of the Report, will show that I entertain a diametrically opposite opinion.*

Sir H. de la Beche embodied his views in chapters, and *gave no distinct classification.*[1] He described the St. Agnes and Crousa Down deposits as supra-Cretaceous; my opinion respecting them is derived from *original observations* made in Cornwall, Dorset, and Somerset; from a *minute survey* of about 800 square miles in Devonshire; and *from the facts, not opinions,* of previous and contemporary observers. By accumulating these materials during several years, I have endeavoured to bridge over the gaps in the chain of Post-Tertiary chronology in Devon and Cornwall occasioned by the general absence of the earlier deposits; but, as negative evidence and reasoning from analogies are, in some cases, the only *modus operandi,* I availed myself of them, and this has laid me open to the charge of entertaining "not very definite" views, brought against me by the Referee, on a subject where very definite views could not be put forward without evoking *imaginary deposits,* or binding myself to hypotheses which, although I have now *strong grounds* for entertaining them, might have to be modified, or possibly abandoned, in the light of future discoveries.

Next, as to my paper on Pleistocene, or Post-Tertiary, phenomena near Padstow. These observations were not included in the larger paper, owing to their *extreme importance.* In *no other part* of the South-Western counties has *so interesting a collection of Pleistocene, or Post-Tertiary, phenomena been observed within so small a space.*

The Referee's remarks on this paper are irrelevant. I have given Mr. Henwood's notes on the Dunbar (Doombar) submerged forest in MSS. for articles in the "Geological Magazine," containing a mass of details not embraced in the papers submitted to the Society. *Mr. Henwood did not observe the old consolidated beach on Dunbar Sands,* which is *exceedingly* interesting, and has, as far as I am aware, never been noticed before.

The Greenway Cliff section is also *exceedingly interesting. If I could find a few more sections resembling it, the Referee would have less cause to find fault with the indefinite parts of my classification.* This observation is quite original; it stands alone; and either of the hypotheses put forward to account for it by me are warranted by the facts.

---

[1] In the second edition of his Geological Manual (1832), p. 159, a distinct classification is given by De la Beche, but its application is restricted to the Plymouth raised beach. This classification resembles mine, and would have been mentioned had I noticed it. Although it is not quite relevant.—May 23, 1879.

As to any objection to the term Pleistocene, I would willingly have altered it to Post-Tertiary, Post-Cretaceous, or some equally suitable title, had such emendation been suggested by the Council on admission of the paper for reading. I trust, Gentlemen, that the above statement of the case may suffice to show that it is impossible for me to allow the papers to appear in the form recommended by the Referee, or with any abridgment whatever.

W. A. E. USSHER.

On March 2nd I was informed that the Council would not reconsider their original determination. On March 3rd I received the MSS. from Mr. Dallas, which I now publish without any alteration, addition, or elision (except as regards the supposed fault in Mr. Pattison's Fowey section).

If the decision of the Referee were taken upon papers prior to their admission for reading, authors would have the option of withdrawing their papers or not in the event of an adverse decision ; and by incorporating my papers with the articles in the " Geological Magazine," I should have been spared this unpalatable preface.

By the present system very few long papers can be done justice to in the brief extracts or abstracts to which the author is obliged to confine himself in reading, so that if such papers be afterward printed in short abstract, it is impossible for any one but the Referee to judge of their contents. Whilst the universal admission of papers for reading tends, on the one hand, to crowd out the longer and more general papers, by placing a hasty observation of an isolated section on a level with the geology of a county ; it entails, on the other, the disagreeable necessity of curtailing lengthy papers, not because they, in any way, transgress the rules laid down for admission *in extenso* to the Society's Journal, but because their publication would cause its expansion beyond the limits which economy prescribes. If a limit as to length were assigned to general papers, and rules so clear and concise laid down that there could be no misconstruction or misconception on the part of the Referee, less scope for occult attacks would be afforded to individuals who, prejudiced perhaps with preconceived notions, may now put their veto on the expression of contrary opinions, and negative questions seen from a different point of view to their own.

Whilst the abstract of a long paper when read may provoke but a partial discussion, the Referee has the power, as in my case, of creating objections against a paper, which could be fairly quashed in discussion, with the questionable satisfaction of knowing that his victim is perfectly defenceless. I have, therefore, availed myself of the only possible means of redress, as I conceive that the suppression of opinions founded on facts and long investigation, and put forward solely to supply a deficiency and arrive at the truth, is very likely to prejudice their subsequent communications, unless (as I think the foregoing correspondence will show) it can be proved that the papers in every way fulfilled the requirements of the rules laid down for the Referee's guidance, and that his recommendation to print them in short abstract must therefore be attributed to ignorance of their contents, and of the well-known work of previous observers in the same field.

If future discoveries should prove the classification I have adopted to be erroneous, they would be none the less welcome for presenting new lights, which, in the present state of the subject, are much to be desired, and for settling the object in view, namely, a true statement of the recent geological vicissitudes experienced by Cornwall, though that statement should necessitate the complete abandonment of my present opinions. The absence of connecting links, and the isolation of the older superficial deposits in Devon and Cornwall, taught me the value of guarded opinions in the face of doubtful or negative evidence ; and no better proof of the value of waiting on facts can be adduced than the admirable work of Sir H. de la Beche, as embodied in his Report on the Geology of Devon, Cornwall, and West Somerset, which owes its imperishable excellence to the extent and accuracy of his observations, and the discrimination which he displayed in not committing himself to definite opinions where direct evidence was not obtainable.

To conclude, had the Referee simply recommended the printing of the following papers in brief abstract on account of their length and the number of quotations, I should have printed them without this preface, which is written in vindication of my work, and in answer to objections which I should hardly have deemed worthy a reply had they been urged in discussion.   W. A. E. U.

PART I.

THE PLEISTOCENE[1] DEPOSITS OF CORNWALL.

INTRODUCTION.

NOTWITHSTANDING the excellent observations of Messrs. Boase, Carne, Henwood, and others, which afford plentiful material for a connected history of the later part of the Pleistocene period in Cornwall, such an attempt has not hitherto been made.

With the intention of supplying this want, I visited Cornwall in the summer of 1876, carefully observing the coast-line as far as practicable in the following districts. From Polkerris, near Par, to Coverack Cove in the Lizard district; thence over Goonhilly Downs to Mullion; from Mullion to Penzance; from St. Loy Cove to the Logan Rock; from Cape Cornwall to the Land's End; from St. Ives to Godrevy Island; St. Agnes Beacon; from Porth Towan (to the south of Perran Sands) to Tintagel. A thorough survey of the inland districts, with which I am unacquainted, would, doubtless, furnish a very valuable addition to the inquiry, notwithstanding the numerous facts accumulated, selections from which are alone given in this paper, so far as they are necessary to establish the conclusions embodied in the Second Part (Classification).

The early Pleistocene history of Cornwall, like that of Devon, is very obscure. The absence of any records of Boulder-clay, *roches moutonnés*, or striations, gives no colour to the hypothesis that Cornwall was submerged during the Glacial epoch, or that it was invaded by foreign ice. If land-ice helped to mould the contour, it must have been local, and all traces must have been expunged by subsequent subaerial waste. The quartz gravels of Crousa Down and

---

[1] The term Pleistocene is used in an indefinite sense, as the oldest deposits cannot with propriety be included under that name in its ordinary acceptation; but as, with their exception, the phenomena discussed, from Raised Beaches to the present time, are Pleistocene, and with them the classification is principally concerned, no better titles than Pleistocene and Post-Tertiary occurred to me.—W. U., Aug. 9th, 1879.

Crowan, and the sands and clays of St. Agnes, are the oldest deposits
on record, and might be even referred to the Tertiary period.
Between these and the Raised Beaches, with which the unbroken
record commences, save in occasional Boulder-gravels at high levels,
we have no connecting links. The numerous excellent examples of
Raised Beaches and stony loam, or ' Head,' which Cornwall affords,
owing to the greater extent of its Palæozoic coast-line, and the completeness of the stream-tin sections, not only make the Pleistocene
history of Cornwall more interesting than that of Devon, but to a
certain extent make up for the absence of cavern deposits. As it is
not possible to treat deposits of different ages, when associated in
the same sections, separately, I have noticed Head and Raised
Beaches together, and embraced under the head of stream-tin the
deposits overlying the submerged forests, reserving the last place
for a brief notice of Blown Sands and Gravel Bars. In the second
part of the paper I propose to weave these materials into chronological order.

OLDEST DEPOSITS.

Crousa Down Gravel.

Upon Crousa Down, in the Lizard District, a patch of quartz
gravel occurs at a height of about 360 feet above the sea, or about
20 feet lower than Roskruge Beacon. The ground is nearly level,
with a slight slope toward the south. It has been described by the
Rev. E. Budge.[1] I obtained the following section of the gravel pits,
which are from six to twelve feet in depth:

1. Brown earthy soil, with angular stones and pebbles of quartz,
   lying unevenly upon ... . 1ft. to 4ft.
2. Reddish-brown earthy sand, with angular fragments of quartz ⎱
3. Light-brown and grey clay, containing patches of fine quartz ⎰ 6ft.
   gravel and loamy sand in places ... ...

Below this the section was concealed by talus. The base of the
gravel is not shown; the sides of two ponds at the bottom of the
pits are composed of quartz gravel.

On the opposite side of the pit to the foregoing, the deposit is
represented by quartz gravel of irregular pebbles and subangular
fragments, those of small size predominating, in brownish loam,
exhibiting no signs of bedding. On some parts of Crousa Down

[1] Trans. Roy. Geol. Soc. Corn. vol. vi. pp. 1 and 91.

the surface is studded with diallage boulders. Near Cowissack I noticed that the boulders rested on soil of drab and light-brown sandy loam, with small angular pieces of quartz, which was exposed by a pond to the depth of one foot.

Mr. Budge[1] says: "The whole country from Porthoustock to Gwinter, four miles, is strewn with a broad band of scattered boulders of a rock locally called Ironstone. A little to the west of Cronsa Down a stratum, commonly termed Marle, of decomposed syenitic rock of the same character as the boulders on the Down, is met with."

Quartz Gravel in the Parish of Crowan.

Mr. Tyack[2] notices the occurrence of quartz pebbles (evidently derived from veins in the Killas) resting on granite, near Polcrebo, in the parish of Crowan, at about 400 feet above the sea, and about 150 feet lower than the lowest part of the adjacent watershed, which separates the basins of the rivers Cober and Hayle. The pebbles vary from the size of a pumpkin to that of a hazel nut; they are less rounded than beach pebbles, but more worn than those in the river gravels of the neighbourhood. The pebbles occur in surface soil, and in a subsoil of yellow clay, resulting from decomposition of granite; the larger pebbles have been found here and there in the clay subsoil, in pits sunk to depths of from two to eight feet. The area covered by the gravel is about 800 yards from north to south, and 500 from east to west. The neighbouring granite hills rise at least 100 feet higher than the site of the gravel, but it occurs at a greater elevation " than any clay slate anywhere near it." In the valley below the gravel patch, and one mile distant from it, similar pebbles have been found mixed with refuse from the stream-tin works.

Between Trewavas Head and Porthleven.

South of Tremearne houses, I noticed five feet of drab loamy clay or earthy soil, with small angular slate fragments, and containing near the surface numerous small well-rounded and smoothed flint and quartz pebbles. The pebbles are found in brown earthy top soil, for five chains eastward from a little stream which trickles

---

[1] Trans. Roy. Geol. Soc. Corn. vol. vi. p. 95.
[2] Trans. Roy. Geol. Soc. Corn. vol. ix. part 2, p. 177, etc.

down the cliff face. From the height of the cliffs it is very unlikely
that these pebbles should have been hurled up by storm waves and
spray from time to time from the beach below; and as there is no
reason to suppose that they were brought to their present site by
human agency, I am inclined to regard them as relics of an old
gravel deposit, perhaps roughly contemporaneous with the gravels
of Crousa Down and Crowan.

Sands and Clays of St. Agnes.

St. Agnes Beacon is encircled on three sides by a deposit of sand
and clay, generally resting on stream-tin, and covered on the surface
by stony clay. This deposit occurs at more than 360 feet above the
sea, and rests on slate, except on the east of the Beacon, where an
isolated patch rests upon granite. De la Beche[1] gives a section of
the deposits. Dr. Boase[2] another. Mr. Hawkins[3] gives four sections
of pits at 375 feet above spring-tide high-water. Mr. Henwood[4]
gives a section, and quotes four others given by Mr. Thomas at
heights of 383, 377, and 418 feet above high-water. The most
complete set of observations is given in a paper by Messrs. Kitto and
Davies,[5] accompanied by a map. A year previous to the publication
of this paper, Mr. Robt. Hunt, F.R.S., Keeper of the Mining Records,
kindly lent me ten sections of the St. Agnes deposits, beautifully
executed by Mr. A. T. Davies; also a map. In Mr. Davies' paper I
find six of these sections given without illustrations. I have reduced
the following four sections from Mr. Davies' illustrations. (See
Plate.) The details of those marked C and E are not given in Mr.
Davies' paper; section F is noticed, and corresponds to H on the
map accompanying the paper; while section A corresponds to J on
the paper, being taken in the isolated patch on the granite where
the clays attain their maximum thickness.

(PLATE, FIG. 1.) Section A, 24 chains distant from the Beacon
in the direction of W. 18° S.

Soil and overburden	9ft. 1in.
Candle clay	19ft. 7in.
Pebbles, boulders, and sand, with a seam of sandstone	5ft. 2in.
Upon waterworn granite.	

[1] Report on Geol. of Corn. and Devon, p. 260.
[2] Trans. Roy. Geol. Soc. Corn. vol. iv. p. 296.
[3] Ibid. p. 135, etc. [4] Ibid. vol. v.
[5] Ibid. vol. ix. part 3, p. 196, etc.

(PLATE, FIG. 2.) Section C is nearly 45 chains from the Beacon, in the direction of N. 29° W.

Soil and overburden	5ft. 9in.
Sandy overburden	1ft. 1in.
Fire clay	6ft. 2in.
Sand	7ft. 0in.
Sandstone on sand	2ft. 0in.
Waterworn rock.	

(PLATE, FIG. 3.) Section E is 41 chains from the Beacon, in the direction of N. 11° E.

Soil and overburden	6ft. 10in.
Candle clay	1ft. 8in.
Sand	14ft. 8in.
Sandstone	5ft. 10in.
Sand	0ft. 4in.
On waterworn rock.	

(PLATE, FIG. 4.) Section F is 16½ chains from the Beacon, in the direction of N. 9° E. It shows a cliff as laid open in mining operations at Wheal Coit. The cliff facing north was first exposed, and a level was then driven into it southwards (dotted line), when sand was again found. "From which," says Mr. Davies, "it may be concluded that we have here a wedge-shaped promontory from the main cliff to the west."

Soil	2ft. 0in.
Overburden	20ft. 0in.
Bluish-grey candle clay	0 to 2ft. 0in.
Sand, with pebbles and boulders of granite and stream tin ore	2 to 7ft. 0in.
On waterworn Killas rock.	

The candle clay is bluish, plastic, adhesive, and very tough. The fire clay is bluish or yellowish, is coarse through admixture of sand and gravel, but yields candle clay when well washed. The sand is nearly pure silica, the grains being perfectly rounded and polished. Its colour is in most cases removable by washing. The sandstone is produced by cementing oxide of iron, and occurs sometimes in cores with a sand centre, sometimes in flat uneven layers. The pebbles vary from the size of a hazel nut to large boulders "weighing a ton or more." They are all from local rocks, and "vary with the different districts, and may often be referred to the rock above which they lie."

The variability and impersistence of the beds may be still further seen from the following sections, which I obtained on the occasion of my visit.

(FIG. 5.) Pit No. 1. Distant from the Beacon more than 40 chains, in direction W. 39° N. In one part we have :—

Blackish sandy soil with angular stones	1ft.	0in.
Reddish and yellowish-brown sandy loam, full of angular fragments of grit and quartz	1ft.	6in.
Loamy sand, red	0ft.	6in.
Bluish-grey and brownish loamy sand, occasionally containing small angular fragments of dark-grey slate, and quartz, passing horizontally into	0 to 2ft.	0in.
Fine bluish-grey sand	3 to 4ft.	0in.
Drab and yellowish loam	2ft.	0in.
Stiff light-drab clay, passing downwards into	1ft.	0in.
Orange and yellow sand, not penetrated.		

(FIG. 6.) Pit No. 1. In another part, where the section is about 9 feet in depth.

Red-brown loam, with angular stones: of a lighter colour and with fewer and smaller fragments at (a¹); drab-coloured at (a²). Greenish and drab-grey, tough sandy loam, containing, at (xx), bluish-grey, impersistent, slightly clayey, bands; fine bluish-grey sand, with small angular stones of quartz, and dark-grey slate, here and there.

In another part of the pit :

Brownish and grey clay	3ft.	0in.
Stiff bluish clay, with a thin band of granitic sand near the top	4ft.	0in.
Fine orange sand, yellowish in places, compact, exposed to a depth of	2ft.	0in.

FIG. 5. Pit No. 1.
Vertical Scale 1 in. = 12 ft.   FIG. 7. Pit No 2.

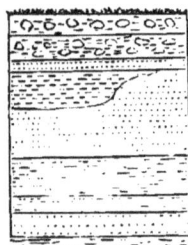

FIG. 6. Pit No. 1.

(FIG. 7.) Pit No. 2 is about 45 chains from the Beacon, in a direction N. 39° W. The section is about 10 feet in depth :

Blackish sandy soil, with angular stones.
Dark-brown sand with small yellowish-red spots in places.
Yellowish and orange sand.
Buff and grey sand.
Light-brown sand.
Impersistent seam of bluish-grey clay.
The colours of the sands merge insensibly into one another.

(FIG. 8.) Pit No. 3 is about 50 chains N. 25° W. from the Beacon :

a. Brown clay with angular stones.
b. Dark reddish-brown clay and loam, with angular stones.
c. Orange, bright reddish, and yellow, fine sand.
(a, b, and c dovetail, a being above, and c below.)
d. Grey and light bluish-grey clay, loamy in places, and of a light
brown tinge toward the base, about four feet thick.
e. Fine light-grey sand, about four feet thick.
f. Fine gamboge-coloured sand, orange in places, not penetrated.

(FIG. 9.) Pit No. 4 is about 47 chains N. 6° E. from the Beacon :

Grey and blackish soil, with small angular stones, yellowish at
the base   ...   .   1ft.   0in.
Brown loam, with angular stones resting irregularly on buff and
light-yellow fine sand, with angular fragments of slaty grit,
sometimes of large size   ...   .   6ft.   0in.

FIG. 8.   Pit No. 3.

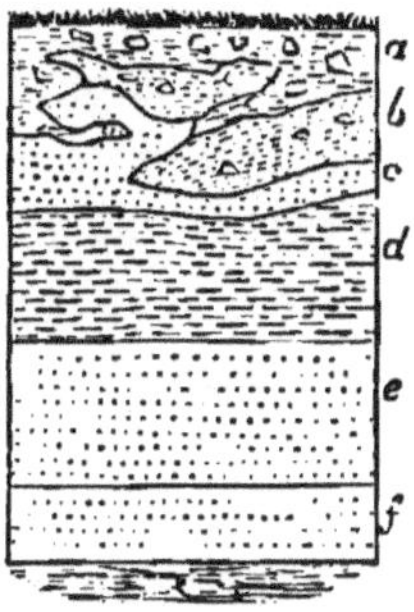

FIG. 9.   Pit No. 4.

BOULDER BEDS.

Mr. Henwood[1] mentioned the occurrence of boulders at Morrab
Place, in Penzance, at 80 feet above the sea-level.   At Lamorna
Cove, Mr. Carne[2] noticed boulders of immense size in the roof of a
cavern ten feet above the highest tide.   Between Lamorna Cove and
Mousehole he observed three to eight feet of boulders under 30
feet of angular fragments in clay, to the north-west of Carndu.

Near Carn Bargis he noticed a mixture of boulders and angular
fragments, about 20 feet above high-tide level.   The roof of Gamper
Hole is composed of granite boulders, under 20 feet of granite fragments in clay, and is 40 feet above high-tide level.

[1] Trans. Roy. Geol. Soc. Corn. vol. v. p. 112.
[2] *Ibid.* vol iii. p. 229, etc.

At Pedn-men-du Mr. Carne observed a few boulders at 30 feet above the sea. The same observer records the occurrence of a bed of boulders 15 feet thick, in a disintegrated granite and clay matrix, at 50 feet from the surface, and about 500 feet above the sea, in sinking a shaft at Huel Carn tin mine. No boulders were found in the lode.

Mr. Salmon mentioned the discovery of granite boulders at 74 fathoms from the surface in West Rosewarne Mine, Gwinear, which he thought had been introduced by fissures from the surface.

At Relistan Mine Mr. Carne mentioned the occurrence of a mass of slate pebbles at 100 fathoms from the surface, but he commented on the presence of spheroidal concretions in the slates in the vicinity.

Mr. Whitley[1] gives a sketch section from Zennor Castle to the coast on the north of it, showing boulders of granite on the surface of a bed of decomposed granitic loam, thin on the slope, but as much as 10 feet thick on level ground, and resting alike on granite and killas. Though the above may be due to early Pleistocene denudation, it is more probably ascribable to the period during which the Head was accumulated. Diallage boulders are similarly separated by soil from their parent rock in the Lizard District.

RAISED BEACHES AND HEAD.

In the garden of a house by Par Harbour, near Spit Point, I observed gravel (composed of small rounded pebbles of quartzite and granitic rocks, generally of small size, with rounded and subangular boulders) and beds of greenish grey sand (with reddish streaks and fragments of shale), about 6 feet in thickness, and 8 feet above high-water mark at its base.

On the north side of Spit Point, I obtained the following section:

Brown sandy soil: gravel of pebbles, principally quartz	4ft.	0in.
Brown gravel finer than the above: gravel with boulders	3ft.	0in.
Grey loam with quartz pebbles	1ft.	0in.
resting on slates at 8 feet above the present beach.		

On the south of Spit Point the base of the gravel is about 10 feet above high-water mark.

[1] Journ. Roy. Inst. Corn. No. 11, p. 184.

(Fig. 10.) Gerran's Bay. The base of the Raised Beach is only a foot or two above the reach of spring-tides in some spots, although its average elevation is between 5 and 15 feet above high-water mark.

In one place the section consists of:

Brown loam with angular stones of slate and quartz	10 to 15ft.
Orange-coloured sand or loam	1ft.
Reddish-brown sand with coarse and fine quartz gravel, and angular fragments of slaty rock, sometimes of large size ...	6ft.

Fig. 10. Gerran's Bay. Vertical Height of Cliff, 25 to 30 feet.

Near Pendowa, the beach is absent, and the angular accumulation rests directly upon the slates.

Falmouth. To the west of Pendennis Point, Head of flattish angular slate fragments and large angular pieces of quartz in grey loam, becoming reddish-brown near the base, rests upon—light yellowish-brown loamy clay, containing a few small angular stones on—dark-grey slates with quartz veins.

South of the Falmouth Hotel.

Under Head, traces of a beach or old river gravel of quartz pebbles in a brown and blackish sandy matrix, consolidated in places, rest on a waterworn rock platform at from 3 to 6 feet above high-water mark.

Between the above and Swanpool Point, a bed of quartz pebbles, 2 feet in thickness, rests on slates at about 10 feet above high-water mark.

Near Bream, to the south of Maen Porth, under stony loam, 4 feet of blackish and brown sand, with angular slate fragments, is exposed in the cliffs at from 10 to 15 feet above high-water mark. Reefs of

2

rock in the vicinity exhibit planed surfaces at about 6 feet above high-water mark, being probably remnants of the old beach bed.

During the accumulation of the Head in this section, the beach appears to have been mixed with it.

In the Cove near Rosemullion Head, to the south of Bream, the cliffs exhibit—Head of yellowish and brown loam, with angular stones, on—blackish and brown sand, with quartz pebbles, 4 to 5 feet in thickness, and from 5 to 10 feet above high-water mark.

In Coverack Cove, the cliff to the north of the village is composed of brown earthy sand with angular stones (the distribution of which gives an appearance of bedding), upon—sand, with pebbles and boulders of the neighbouring rocks, at base about 8 feet above high-water mark. To the north of the above, 5 to 12 feet of buff and greyish loamy sand, with iron-stained bands, contains pebbles and boulders, in places, at its base from 5 to 10 feet above high-water mark.

In Porthbeer Cove, to the south of Coverack, pebbles and large boulders of diallage rock, and occasional small flints, in brownish earthy loam, occur at about 10 feet above high-water mark. The face of the low cliffs is composed of brownish sand, probably blown against them.

Between Trewavas Head and Porthleven, south of Tremearne houses, the cliff section shows :

Grey loamy soil, with flint and quartz pebbles	2ft.
Grey loam, with angular slate and granite fragments of rather small size	3ft. to 5ft.
Grey loam, with angular fragments of slate and granite, and rough granite boulders	5ft. to 6ft.

resting upon nearly horizontal grey slates with quartz veins, at from 12ft. to 15ft. above high-water mark.

(FIG. 11.) The low cliffs between Pra and Sydney Cove are composed of Head, with the exception of the upper part, which consists of blown sand 2 to 3 feet in thickness. In one place, where the cliff is about 14 feet in height, a trace of consolidated blackish sand, made up chiefly of comminuted slate fragments, is visible at the base of the cliffs about 2 feet above high-water mark ; it is overlain by 12 feet of coarse granitic loam, containing angular fragments of slate, granite, and quartz, and some subangular boulders.

Toward Sydney Cove the cliff becomes lower, and the Head

varies, the upper part, for 4 feet, consisting of yellowish loam, with small angular stones unequally distributed, upon—5 feet of brown loam, with small angular fragments of slate, and larger angular slate, quartz, and occasionally elvan, stones. A few small flint and quartz pebbles and angular stones are visible in a grey sandy top soil.

FIG. 11. PRA SANDS.

Vertical Scale—1 inch = 96 feet. Horizontal Scale—5 inches = 1 mile.

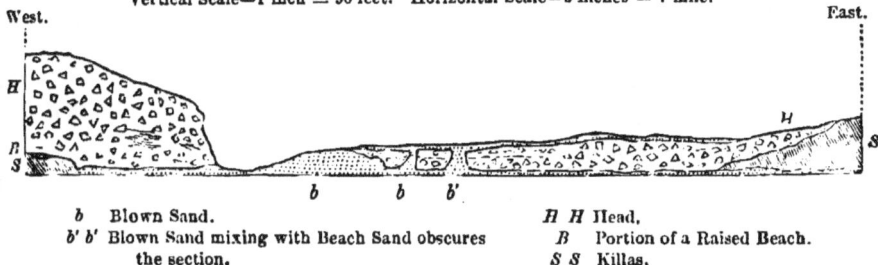

b	Blown Sand.	H H	Head.
b' b'	Blown Sand mixing with Beach Sand obscures the section.	B	Portion of a Raised Beach.
		S S	Killas.

The cliffs to the west of Sydney Cove are composed of Head, brown loamy clay, with angular fragments of slate and granite, containing seams of brown clay with fewer stones, and passing into stiff drab clay at the base of the cliff.

Near the above the cliffs are about 50 feet in height, and composed entirely of greyish-brown loam and clay, with angular fragments of granite and slate.

On a little promontory near the above, a trace of Raised Beach is visible; it consists of 4 feet of reddish quartzose loamy sand, containing pebbles, subangular slate boulders, and angular and subangular fragments of quartz and slate. The base of the deposit is about 5 feet above high-water mark; it is capped by 10 feet of Head, grey loam, with angular fragments. In another spot drab clay overlies 2 feet of pebbles and angular and subangular fragments.

At Trevean Cove the cliff presents the following section :

Grey and brownish loam, containing angular stones (not of the subjacent slates), occasionally presenting a stratified appearance with a seaward inclination...	8ft.	6in.
Coarse blackish and grey sand with quartz pebbles, and subangular fragments, also large subangular boulders of greenstone, one of which measured 5ft. by 2ft. 6in. by 2ft.	4ft.	0in.

A small piece of a broken flint pebble was obtained from this bed. The base of the deposit is from 5 to 8 feet above high-water mark.

The following section was obtained in the cliffs to the south of
Perranuthno :

> Head of angular greenstone fragments in loam, in places stained
> reddish, and with few stones toward the base, upon—fine quartz
> gravel, or coarse waterworn sand mixed with earthy matter
> from the Head above, 5 feet thick, and, at base, about 8 feet
> above high-water mark.

Near the above, under Head as before :

> Coarse sand with earthy matter, cemented by iron into nodular
> pieces ... ...   1ft. 6in.
> Coarse sand, cemented in veins by iron   ... ...   6in.
> Coarse sand or fine gravel, chiefly composed of quartz; grit,
> slate and flint being also present; containing angular and sub-
> angular fragments of quartz and greenstone ... ...   3ft. 6in.

The base of the deposit is from 8 to 10 feet above high-water
mark.

(FIG. 12.)   In St. Loy Cove, south of St. Buryan, to the east of
the stream, the cliff section consists of :

> Angular and subangular blocks of granite and stones of quartz,
> slate and fine slaty grit in brown sandy loam .. ..   10ft. to 15ft.
> Yellowish-brown loam, with angular stones and pebbles, of
> granite, grit, and quartz, presenting an appearance of
> irregular bedding   ... ...   2ft.
> Coarse angular granitic sand (Growan), with large rounded
> granite boulders and pebbles of quartz, dark-bluish slate,
> granite, etc. At base, about 10 feet above high-water mark...   4ft.

FIG. 12. ST. LOY COVE. 1 inch = 24 feet.

Land's End District.

In Sennen Cove, Whitesand Bay, here and there at the base of the
low cliffs, pebbles are visible under stony loam ; in one place a trace
of black, consolidated coarse sand binds two boulders of granite, at

about high-water mark. It is possible that this may be a relic of a raised beach, destroyed at a higher level.

Between Pornanvon and Pol Pry, near the latter, the following section was shown in the cliff :

Large granite boulders in soil ... ...

Yellowish-brown, coarse granitic *débris* (Growan) with large
 angular fragments ... ... 15ft.

As above, with great angular boulders, and small fragments of
 schorlaceous and porphyritic granite. The matrix becomes
 darker in the lower part, and for 5 feet upward from its base,
 exhibits an appearance resembling false bedding ... ... 25ft.

Granite boulders, round and subangular, with a few pebbles of
 dark bluish-grey slate, resting upon decomposing granite, at
 from 10 to 20 feet above high-water mark ... ... 2ft. to 5ft.

(Fɪɢ. 13.) Pornanvon Cove. The cliffs near the mouth of the stream give the following section :

Head, of angular fragments of granite, some of great size, in
 coarse granitic *débris* (Growan)... ... ... 20ft.

Large granite boulders, smooth and well rounded, lying irregularly on granite which in one place separates the bed altogether 5ft. to 15ft.

Fɪɢ. 13. Pornanvon. 1 inch = 32 feet.

The base of the boulder bed is from 5 to 15 feet above high-water mark ; occasional smaller pebbles of slate and quartz occur in it.

In Priest Cove the following cliff section was obtained :

Head, of light-brown loam, with angular slate, and, occasionally,
 granitic fragments, becoming darker in colour, and containing
 fewer stones for from 5 to 10 feet from its base ... ... 10ft. to 15ft.

Blackish and brown coarse earthy sand ... ... 6in. to 1ft.

Gravel, chiefly composed of pebbles of altered slate, greenstone,
 quartz, and, occasionally, flint ... ... 3in. to 2ft.

At base 5 to 10 feet above high-water mark.

The following section was obtained from the cliffs, near Cape Cornwall.

Brown loam, with numerous angular fragments	12ft. 0in.
Impersistent band of blackish loam	0ft. 6in.
Dark-brown loam, with fewer angular stones than the upper bed	5ft. 0in.
Brownish-yellow sandy loam, with a few angular fragments ...	1ft. 0in.
Brownish sandy loam, with angular fragments, and pebbles of quartz, slate, and greenstone, and boulders near its base which is in places on the level of the present beach	4ft. 0in.

Head is shown on a rock isolated from the cliffs, near Cape Cornwall. Mr. Carne [1] describes a Raised Beach in Treen Cove, to the east of Gurnard's Head Promontory, near St. Ives, composed of pebbles and boulders of the subjacent rock of various sizes, in clayey and sandy matrixes; about 60 yards in length, 15 feet in thickness, 20 feet above spring-tide high-water; and overlain by Head, earthy clay with angular fragments.

(Fig. 14.) St. Ives. Cliff sections in Porthgwidden Cove, under Head, of light brown and yellowish brown loam, from 5 to 15 feet thick, shown in the north part of the cove.

Yellowish-brown loam	3ft.
Pebbles of grit, quartz, slate, and, occasionally, flint	3ft. to 6ft.

Fig. 14. Porthgwidden Cove, St. Ives.
1 inch = 24 feet.

In another part of the Cove:

Quartz, slate, grit, greenstone, and, occasionally, flint pebbles in yellowish-brown sand	4ft. 0in.
Strip of rather fine yellowish sand...	4in. to 6in.
Quartz, grit, slate, and occasional flint and granite pebbles in yellowish-brown sand	3ft. to 4ft.

The base of the pebble deposits is about 5 feet above high-water mark.

[1] T. R. G. S. Corn. vol. vii. p. 176.

The cliffs from a point west of Gwythian to Godrevy Island exhibit a very fine example of a raised beach, at base from 5 to 8 feet above high-water mark.

In one spot, west of Gwythian, the low cliff consists of:

Blown sand	2ft.	0in.
Brown sand	5ft.	0in.
Gravel of grit, slate, quartz, and a few flint pebbles near the base, at about 5 feet above high-water mark; coarse black consolidated sand, containing pebbles, fills up the inequalities in the subjacent grey slate platform	2ft.	0in.

(FIG. 15.) At nearly three-quarters of a mile to the south of Godrevy Island, I obtained the following section:

1. Head, of light-brown and grey loam, with angular fragments. stained blackish at the base ... ...   15ft.
2. Brown and drab iron-stained sand, with bands of pebbles in places 10ft. to 15ft.
3. Pebbles of quartz and slate, of various sizes, with subangular fragments of slate in coarse sand, consolidated near the base in which a large boulder was noticed. Base of pebbles, 5 feet above high-water mark ... ...   1ft. to 5ft.

FIG. 15. GODREVY CLIFFS looking toward Gwythian.

Vertical height represented in foreground = 34 feet.

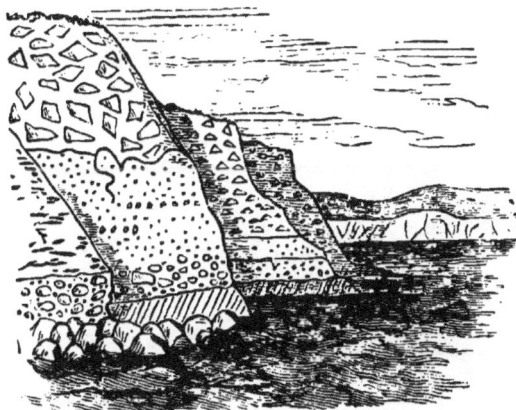

Near the above the old consolidated pebble beach forms the roof of cavernous hollows in the slates in two places. Where the consolidated sand beds attain their maximum development near Godrevy Island, the section consists of :

Brown loam, with angular stones	5ft.	0in.
Coarse grey and buff consolidated sand, with angular grains, in beds apparently dipping inland. (Probably old blown sand.)	10ft.	0in.
Coarse grey sand, with pebbles scattered through it, and traversed by a line of pebbles	6ft.	0in.
Coarse sand of quartz grains and comminuted shells, full of quartz and slate pebbles and subangular fragments, and containing a few pieces of flint ; a fragment of a *Murex* was also obtained...	3ft. to 4ft.	

The base of the deposit is about 4 feet above high-water mark.

Rock platforms abound on this coast, their surfaces being planed at about the level of spring-tide high-water.

(Fig. 16.) Near the point where the foregoing section was obtained, a reef of rocks is noticeable at 70 yards from the cliffs, and is capped by a pinnacle of Head, consisting of light-brown loam with angular slate fragments. Just below the Head traces of reddish and black consolidated sand fill up inequalities in the reef, at about 10 feet above high-water mark. A pebble bed, at base not much above high-water mark, occurs under Head, capped by blown sand in the adjacent cliffs.

Fig. 16. On Godrevy Beach.

Rock Reef 70 yards from the Cliffs, bearing traces of Raised Beach and capped by a Pinnacle of Head.

(FIG. 17.) Fistral Bay. General section:

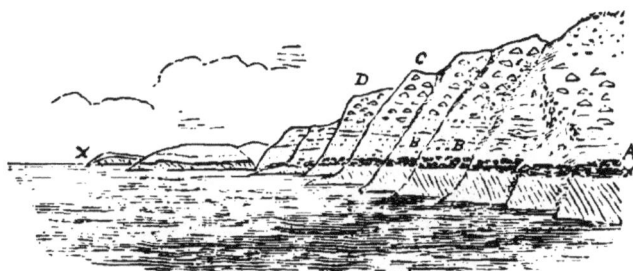

FIG. 17. FISTRAL BAY.

A. Pebbles of slate and quartz in coarse black consolidated sand.
BB. Boulders of quartz in the pebble bed A.
C. Cliff section—Angular quartz stones in sand and loam, upon—10 feet of sand and gravel, upon—2 feet of gravel.
D. Cliff section—Head—upon coarse brownish consolidated sand beds, upon —pebbles in black consolidated sand.
xx. Line of Raised Beach, base about 5 feet above high-water-mark.

The following sections have been selected out of many observations which I made of the cliffs in Fistral Bay. Near the centre of the Bay, under Head:

Coarse consolidated sand	1ft.	0in.
Quartz pebbles	0ft.	6in.
Coarse consolidated sand	1ft.	6in.
Sand, with numerous small pieces of slate	1ft.	6in.
Coarse consolidated sand	2ft.	0in.
Coarse black sand, with bands of gravel, of pebbles, and sub-angular fragments of quartz and slate ; occasional boulders near its base, which is from 5 to 6 feet above high-water mark	3ft.	0in.

Near the north end of the bay, loam with angular slate fragments rests on beds of consolidated sand, which appear to overlie—a Head of angular fragments with occasional pebbles, resting on—the Raised Beach sand and gravel.

In this case the old blown sand seems to have accumulated upon talus resting on the Raised Beach prior to the formation of the Head above.

(FIG. 18.) At Towan Head, on the north of Fistral Bay:

Coarse brown consolidated sand beds, with a seaward dip of about 15°	6ft.	0in.
Coarse brown consolidated sand, with large angular and sub-angular fragments and pebbles of quartz, slate, and granite ...	2ft.	6in.
Fine gravel, chiefly composed of quartz pebbles, containing large angular fragments of slate	1ft.	0in.

At base, from 5 to 6 feet above high-water mark.

Near New Quay Pier, a raised beach occurs on a rocky platform about 20 yards in width, and from 5 to 6 feet above high-water mark. It con-

Fig. 18. Towan Head.
Vertical Scale—1 inch = 20 feet.

sists of tough, buff, sand rock, weathering dark grey (frequently emitting sparks when struck), containing large slate and limestone boulders, quartz, slate, and, occasionally, flint pebbles. The boulders might have fallen from cliffs overhanging the old beach during its formation.

Consolidated sand beds (old blown sands) are visible in the adjacent cliffs. Bones of oxen are said to have been found in the consolidated sands of New Quay.[1]

De la Beche says that the consolidated sands of New Quay are sometimes cemented by oxide of iron or calcareous matter, and sometimes by both.[2] In the Fistral Bay raised beach, Mr. S. R. Pattison[3] found *Modiola vulgaris, Cytherea chione, Patella, Ostrea.*

(Fig. 19). Constantine Island is capped by brown sand, with tests of *Patellæ* and broken *Mytili* to a depth of from 1 to 2 feet; under which, toward the north part of the island, angular fragments of slate and quartz, and occasionally greenstone pebbles, are shown, forming an impersistent bed 3 feet in maximum thickness, and at base, from 5 to 8 feet above high-water mark.

Fig. 19. Constantine Island.
1 inch = 24 feet.

[1] From the small quantity of sand now drifted on the old consolidated sand dunes of New Quay, De la Beche considered that the change of level had rendered the locality less fit for such accumulations than it was during the Raised Beach formation.—De la Beche, Report on the Geology of Cornwall and Devon, p. 428.
[2] *Ibid.* p. 431.
[3] Trans. Roy. Geol. Soc. Corn. vol. vii. p. 50.

STREAM-TIN SECTIONS.

The records of stream-tin sections are so numerous and interesting that it is difficult to make a selection without giving the stock instances of Par and Pentuan and Carnon; these, as well as some interesting sections given by Mr. Henwood, in which probably contemporaneous beds are marked, have been omitted through want of space, and a host of lesser sections are represented by samples here and there.

(FIG. 20). By Mr. S. R. Pattison.[1] Fowey Valley Works :

FIG. 20. FOWEY VALLEY WORKS.

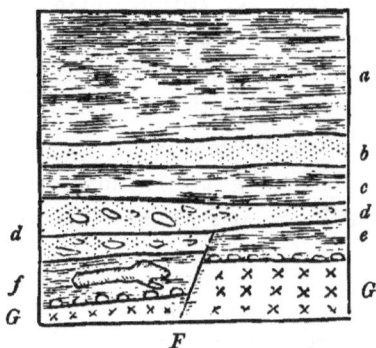

a. Peat ... ... 14ft. 0in.
b. Fine washed sand ... ... 2ft. to 3ft.
c. Peat, containing wood, ferns, bazel nuts, etc., well preserved,
    also the horns of deer... ... ... 4ft. to 5ft.
d. Sand and rounded stones, with much tin... ... ... 1ft. to 7ft.
e. Peat, very hard and black, containing numerous trees, etc. ... 3ft. 0in.
f. Peat, with a large tree trunk, found in June, 1847.
G. Granite shelf, on which large quantities of tin were found.
F. Possible fault, downthrow 5 feet, lined with small quartz
    crystals. [Mr. Pattison has since informed me that he is in-
    clined to refer this faulted appearance to unequal erosion of the
    shelf at a quartz vein.]

Par and Pentuan.

In a shaft in the lower ground, near Par Estuary, a bed of sea sand 4 feet thick, containing shells, was met with at 16 feet 6 inches from the surface, between two beds containing traces of vegetation mixed with *débris*. The description[2] of this section is not suffi-

---

[1] Trans. Roy. Geol. Soc Corn. vol. vii. p. 34.
[2] Report on the Geology of Cornwall and Devon, p. 403.

ciently definite to enable one to make a rough correlation with the beds given in Mr. Colenso's section [1] of the Happy Union Works, Pentuan, where a bed of sea sand with shells, 4 inches thick, occurs between beds containing forest remains, at 42 feet from the surface; but in the uppermost bed, 20 feet thick, sea sand is intercalated with river sediments; and a row of wooden piles was met with, their tops being 24 feet from the surface, and on a level with spring-tide low-water mark. Mr. Henwood [2] says that the tin ground in Pentuan Works, near the sea, is below the sea-level and covered by sea sand and shells, whilst in the stream works higher up the valley, the tin ground rests on granite, and is covered by recent alluvia.

Mr. Rashleigh described [3] the stream works of Poth and Sandry-cock, in the valley between St. Austell and St. Blazey. The vale has so gentle a slope that, but for a flood hatch, the salt water would flow into Poth. It opens into the Par Estuary, the level of its basin being considerably below low-water mark. The accumulation of a beach bar prevents the sea from going up the moor, except by the adit.

Section of Stream Works at Poth, near the sea, and Sandrycock, near the middle of the vale.

1. Vegetable mould ... ... about	0ft.	3in.
2. Gravel and micaceous sand, mixed with loam in alternate beds	8ft.	3in.
3. Light-coloured clay with a little mica, with traces of decaying roots	5ft.	3in.
4. Black peat	4ft.	1in.
5. Light-coloured clay	1ft.	4in.
6. Stiff light-brown clay, with light-bluish spots, containing decayed vegetable matter	3ft.	10in.
7. Sea sand and clay mixed	3ft.	0in.
8. Very fine micaceous sea sand, with comminuted shells and bits of slate	4ft.	0in.
9. Coarser sand without shells	6ft.	0in.
10. Solid black fen, with few vegetable remains (not used for fuel)	2ft.	10in.
11. Tin ground and loose stones of various kinds	1ft. to 6ft.	
12. Killas, on which tin ground and in some places yellow clay rests		

At Poth, near the bottom of the sea sand, and upon the sea mud, horns of deer and wild oxen were found. A pair of the latter measured 15 inches in circumference at the base.

[1] *Ibid.* pp. 401, 402, 403.
[2] Trans. Roy. Geol. Soc. Corn. vol. v. p. 129.
[3] *Ibid.* vol. ii. pp. 282, 284, 286.

Section at Pendelow. St. Austell Valley[1] Deposits wrought in 1873:

1. Granitic sand and gravel, divided by thin partings of silt into many separate beds .. ..   6ft. to 8ft.
2. Peat (fen) often mixed with and sometimes interlaid by microscopic layers of granitic sand... ... ... $\frac{3}{10}$ft. to 2ft.
3. Granitic sand and gravel in many layers, the lower part being much mixed with hardened mud ... .   7ft. to 8ft.
4. Peat, very closely resembling No. 2... ... ...
5. Granitic sand and clay, scarcely differing from No. 1 ... ...   3in. to 6in.
6. Peat, sometimes mixed with stems of fern, nuts, leaves, branches of furze, alder, and hazel, and trunks of oaks; here and there a few flints have been very rarely discovered ... ...   1ft. 0in.
7. Tin ground, of granitic, schorlaceous and quartzose, matter, mixed with the oxide of tin, usually as sand and gravel, but sometimes including subangular masses of granitic rocks and vein stones, and more rarely thin scales of slate ... ...   2ft. to 4ft.
Upon granite shelf unequally eroded.

Section of Lower Creamy Works,[2] in a part of Red Moor, in Lanlivery. (N. of St. Austell.)

1. Peat ... ...   2ft. to 3ft.
2. Granitic, though slightly quartzose, clay of a greyish hue, mixed with laminæ of slate ... ...   1ft. to 3ft.
3. Tin ground of angular, subangular, and spheroidal masses of pale-brown quartz, fragments of felspar mottled dark blue and yellowish brown, clay and granitic gravel, thinly mixed with rounded masses of tin stone. Flints of considerable size occur at intervals, and particles of gold less frequently ...   4ft. to 5ft.
The roots of marsh plants penetrate to a depth of from 2 to 3 feet into the tin ground.
Shelf of pale-buff coloured clay.

The occurrence of flints in the tin ground is remarkable, unless by that name siliceous fragments of Palæozoic rocks are meant. Section of Carnon Works, in 1807, by Mr. E. Smith:[3]

1. Mud and sand ... ...   7ft. 0in.
2. Granitic gravel, with a few shells (charcoal?) ... ...   4ft. 0in.
3. Fine gravel, shells, mud; irregular strata of oysters extend to within 4 or 5 feet of the tin ground ... ...   12ft. 0in.
4. Closer mud, shells, trunks and branches, sometimes exhibiting the appearance of having been cut by an axe; horns and bones of stags, human skulls ... ...   19ft. 0in.
5. Tin ground ... ...   1ft. to 6ft.

[1] Henwood, Journ. Roy. Instit. Corn. vol. iv. p. 213.
[2] *Ibid.* p. 214.
[3] Trans. Roy. Geol. Soc. Corn. vol. iv. p. 408.

Mr. Henwood gives a section of Carnon Works,[1] evidently at some distance from the above, for a bed containing moss, leaves, nuts, wood, oyster shells, animal remains, chiefly cervine, and human skulls; 18 inches thick; rests on the tin ground, and, when traced seaward, gives place to silt, the lowermost bed of the overlying 53 feet of sand, mud, silt and shells.

De la Beche,[2] commenting on these sections, says that the name Carnon applies to a long line of works down the valley, and that the shells in both sections correspond to species now living in the Falmouth Estuary.

At Perranwell, an open work, more than 50 years ago, showed:[3]

1. Angular gravel, sand and silt, with worn masses of granite and slate, in thin beds; deer remains were found at a considerable depth, and still deeper oyster shells ... ... 12ft. to 15ft.
2. Fine silt, mixed with oyster shells, leaves, nuts, branches of trees, and very rarely wing cases of beetles ... ... 6in. to 1ft. 6in.
3. Tin ground, small rounded tin stones, angular and subangular blocks of schorl rock, granite, quartz, quartzose slate, and other vein stones. On shelf of clay slate ... ... 2ft. to 3ft.

In Gwennap,[4] toward the middle of the vale, half-way from Tarnon Dean (? Tannerdane on the map) to the Arsenic Manufactory, large rough angular masses of quartz, two or three tons in weight, rested on a bed of silt, shells, and vegetable matter, at 16 feet below the surface; beneath this, at about 22 feet below high-, and 4 or 5 feet below low-water mark, an entire human skeleton was discovered within the compass of the layer of animal, vegetable, and mineral substances.

Cober Valley to North of the Loo Pool.

Mr. J. Rogers[5] says that in one part of the Cober Valley, 28 feet from the surface and directly superimposed on the tin ground, a vegetable stratum, containing leaves and trunks of trees, also hazel nuts, was met with, there being no indications of vegetable growth in the overlying deposits. At Wheal Cober no indications of marine deposits were found on the Killas; nor at Helston Gas Works, where an excavation was made to a depth of 21 feet, or 7 feet below high-water mark.

[1] Journ. Roy. Instit. Corn. vol. iv.
[2] Report on Geol. of Corn. and Devon, p. 404.
[3] Henwood, Journ. Roy. Instit. Corn. vol. iv.   [4] *Ibid.* p. 206.
[5] Trans. Roy. Geol. Soc. Corn. vol. vii. p. 352.

Drift Moor Works near Newlyn.

Mr. Carne [1] says the tin ground in these works rested on the sides and bottom of a clay-lined basin, on all sides except the north, the point at which alluvial deposits resting on mounds of old workings (carried on to a depth of 36 feet) came in. The tin ground was no thicker at the bottom of the basin, 40 feet from the surface, than on its sides, which are so steep as to come within a foot of it. An old rag and chain pump and three copper coins, one Portuguese, with the figures 169 still legible on it, were found in the alluvial debris, the engine being 15 feet from the surface.

Mr. Carne [2] mentioned some stream tin works at Douran, noticed by Borlase in 1738. The tin ore was pulverized, and occurred under 2 feet of sand and gravel, which becomes 40 feet thick at Douran Hill on the east.

Treloy, in Parish of St. Columb Minor.

De la Beche [3] was informed that the tin ground in the Valley of Treloy rests on an unequal surface; that above the inequality, the tin ground was poor, below it, abundant and mixed with mussel shells, some of which were attached to the rock, as if they had existed prior to the stream-tin formation, at a time when the sea extended up the valley thus far.

Mr. Henwood [4] mentioned the occurrence of a thin bed of tin ore at Treloy, covered by 8 to 10 feet of silt, vegetable matter, sand, and mould, and betraying signs of old workings. Celts, coins, rings, brass brooches were found. The rings were supposed to have been magic rings of the Druids; the coins appeared to be Roman, a slight crystalline incrustation was noticed on one or two of them. In a later paper [5] Mr. Henwood gives the following section of the Treloy works, probably those referred to above:

1. Successive layers of sand and gravel... ... ... 8ft. or 10ft.
2. Vegetable remains ... ... 2in. to 6in.
3. Tin ground... ... ...from 6in. to 2ft.

[1] *Ibid.* vol. iv. p. 47.
[2] *Ibid.* vol. iii. p. 332.
[3] Report on Geol. of Corn. and Devon, p. 405.
[4] Trans. Roy. Geol. Soc. Corn. vol. iv. p. 63.
[5] Journ. Roy. Instit. Corn. vol. iv. p. 219.

He adds: "As every part of this deposit, wrought during the memory of the generation now passing away, was beyond high-water mark at Porth, and even above the level of the Raised Beach at Fistral, near New Quay, it contained neither shell nor other substance of marine origin, but frequently afforded granules of gold." The shelf consists of clay slate.

If De la Beche was not misinformed, we must suppose that the Treloy Valley was excavated prior to the formation of the Raised Beaches, or that the occurrence he describes occupies a very different site from Mr. Henwood's section. If, however, it lay below high-water mark, we might be justified in considering its formation as subsequent to the submergence of the forests, and refer the tin ground in this valley to a still more modern date.

SUBMERGED FORESTS.

Looe.

Mr. Box[1] noticed the exposure of oak, alder, ash, and elm trees under sand and shingle, below high-water mark, on Millendreath Beach, east of Looe. The trees were imbedded in compact peat, chiefly composed of marsh plants.

Fowey.

Mr. Peach[2] states "that portions of trunks and roots of trees, *in situ*, were exposed at Ready Money, in Fowey Harbour, by a heavy gale of wind; they were rooted in a stiff clay over which leaves, flags, etc., and the elytra of beetles, are found."

Porthmellin (near Meragissy).

Mr. Peach[3] observed roots and parts of stems of trees, *in situ*, on clay, surrounded by alluvial matter containing flags and the elytra of beetles, on Porthmellin Beach, after a heavy gale.

Falmouth.

Mr. E. Claypole[4] notices the occurrence of peat, seldom exposed except at spring-tide low-water, and after heavy south-easterly gales, in the curve of the shore at Gyllyngvaes, Falmouth. The peat

---

[1] Twenty-sixth Ann. Rep. Roy. Instit. Corn. for 1844.
[2] Trans. Roy. Geol. Soc. Corn. vol. vii. p. 12.   [3] *Ibid.* vol. vi.
[4] Proc. Brist. Nat. Soc. vol. v. p. 35, for 1870.

contained trunks of alder, oak, and hazel (the latter frequently with nuts and twigs attached), also apparently yew; and remains of red deer, oxen, human skulls, and cut branches. The peat rested on very tenacious clay, and continued down to low-water mark, being overlain by a quartz pebble beach, rising to the level of the highest spring-tides.

Maen Porth, near Falmouth.

The Rev. J. Rogers [1] observed the roots of an oak in peaty matter, with leaves and roots of Iris pseudacorus beneath the surface of the sand below high-water mark, on Maen Porth Beach. The roots were in clay, resting on the solid rock. Pieces of peat were washed ashore during gales.

Porthleven, West of Loo Pool.

The Rev. J. Rogers [2] mentioned the occurrence of stumps of oak and willow, apparently in situ, imbedded in vegetable mould, under 10 feet of sand, at Porthleven, a little below low-water mark.

Mounts Bay.

The Mounts Bay Submerged Forest has been noticed by Leland; by Dr. Borlase,[3] who says that the trees occurred 300 yards within full sea-mark, and at high tide had at least 12 feet of water over them; by Dr. Boase,[4] who inferred, from the occurrence of nuts and leaves in the vegetable mould, that the submergence had taken place in the autumn. I select Mr. Carne's [5] account as giving the best general description : " A mass of decayed plants, full of small branches, twigs, and leaves, generally of hazel or birch, forming a spongy brown substance, occurs under 4 inches to 1 foot of fine sand, on the east of Penzance, continuing for half a mile from east to west, and being in its most southern parts, as far as ascertained, 20 to 30 feet below spring-tide level. Numerous prostrate tree trunks, amongst which oak was noticed, were imbedded in brownish earth full of woody fibre, beyond the pile of rocks near the Chyandower River."

[1] Trans. Roy. Geol. Soc. Corn. vol. iv. p. 481.
[2] Trans. Roy. Geol. Soc. Corn. vol. i. p. 236.
[3] Trans. Roy. Soc. for 1757, p. 80.
[4] Trans. Roy. Geol. Soc. Corn. vol. iii. p. 131.
[5] Ibid. vol. vi. p. 230.

Further eastward the vegetable bed was 4 feet thick, consisting of branches and twigs of hazel and birch in the upper part, and of leaves and woody fibre in the lower part; it extended to the eastern Cressets rocks.[1]

The vegetable stratum generally rests on clay slates, or on a bluish sand, and in one place on a mass of gravel. At Huel Darlington Mine, in Marazion Marsh, Mr. Carne obtained the following section, in a pit near Marazion River:

1. Slime (? river) gravel, and loose ground	8ft.	0in.
2. Peat, with minute woody fibre (fit for fuel)	4ft.	0in.
3. White sand, with *Cardium edule*	12ft.	0in.
4. Oak and hazel trees lying in all directions; hazel nuts loose and on their branches; a piece of oak, shaped as if for a boat keel	1ft. to 2ft.	
5. Solid hard peat, closer than the upper bed (good for fuel) ...	3ft.	0in.
6. Alluvial tin ground on clay slate rock	4ft.	0in.

In a part of Huel Darlington Mine, where the tin ground was at a higher level, bed 3 of the preceding section rested directly on the tin ground.

Mr. Carne considered bed 4 to be a continuation inland of the Mounts Bay Submerged Forest, the difference in level between them being small.

Traces of submarine forests are said to occur at Perran Porth, St. Columb Porth, and Mawgan Porth.[2]

The forest near Padstow, on Dunbar Sands, has been described by Mr. Henwood.[3]

Mr. S. R. Pattison[4] notes the discovery of 20 feet of soil, between high- and low-water mark, at Maer Lake, near Bude Haven; trees of large size, and roots apparently *in situ* in dark clay, have been found; also a bullock's horn 4 feet long and 18 inches in circumference, and a stag's horn 5 feet in length.

---

[1] Dr. Boase (Trans. Roy. Geol. Soc. Corn. vol. iii. p. 172) describes the forest stratum, traceable on the seaward side of the West Green Sand Bank for 200 yards in width, at low water, from Larrigan rocks to Newlyn, as "trunks and branches of hazel, alder, elm, and oak (with leaves and the elytra of beetles), lying in all directions; the larger trunks lie N.E. and S.W., they are split and frequently perforated by *Pholas dactylus*.

[2] De la Beche, Report on Geology of Cornwall, etc., p. 419.

[3] Fortieth Ann. Rep. Roy. Instit. Corn. for 1858.

[4] Trans Roy. Geol. Soc. Corn. vol. vii. p. 34.

BLOWN SANDS AND GRAVEL AND SAND BARS.

From its more exposed situation the north-western coast-line of Cornwall exhibits by far the most considerable accumulations of blown sand. On either side of the Hayle Estuary, and extending as far north as Godrevy Farm, the lower lands are buried beneath sand dunes. The Perran Sands, in which traces of the ruins of Constantine Chapel are still visible, cover a considerable area, attaining in places to more than 300 feet above the sea-level. To the south of Trevose Head the flat land lying on the west of the Camel Estuary is covered by blown sand; also the low-lying tract on the east side of the estuary, in which St. Enodock's Chapel is situated. Blown sand occurs between the latter spot and Tintagel in several places, but of inconsiderable extent. The old consolidated blown sands of the coast near Gwythian and Godrevy, and in Fistral Bay, etc., show that a similar drift of sand prevailed during the Raised Beach formation. A small patch of sand dunes borders Whitesand Bay near the Land's End; blown sand also caps tolerably high land at Gunwalloe near Mullion, in the Lizard District.

Mr. Boase[1] commented on the absence of documentary evidence, or even popular tradition, of the devastation of considerable tracts of land, and the engulphment of a number of churches by the blown sand: "The particular circumstances of the catastrophe seem to have been already forgotten when Leland visited the place, about 300 years ago; and yet the period of its occurrence could not then have been very remote, because 'the churches' still extant are evidently not of an age much anterior to that of Leland himself." As, however, this devastation was most probably gradual, no sudden influx of sand worthy of record may have taken place.

Blown sand sometimes forms the crest of sand or gravel bars on the south-east coast. In the upper part of the West Green Sand-bank, near Marazion Bridge, Mr. Edmonds[2] discovered numerous land shells to a depth of from 7 to 8 feet from the surface. The

[1] Trans. Roy. Geol. Soc. Corn. vol. ii. p. 141.
[2] *Ibid.* vol. vi. pp. 303, 304.

crest of the bank being 18 feet above high-water mark, proving its
Æolian origin. Dr. Boase [1] gives the following section of the bank:

    1. Granitic sand, of quartz, mica, and hornblende slates, with a
        little tin ore, quartz predominating   ... ... 10ft. 0in.
    2. Gravel, pebbles of hornblende slates from 1 to 3 inches in
        diameter ... . 16ft. 0in.
    Resting on the forest bed, which ranges from 12 to 20 feet
    below high-water mark, and rests on decomposed slates.

The West Green Sandbank is much shortened and greatly diminished
in area, there being evidence [2] to show that in Charles the Second's
time it afforded 36 acres of pasturage, whilst it is now but 2 or
3 acres in extent; a diminution for which the large quantity of sand
abstracted for agricultural purposes [3] does not satisfactorily account.

Gravel and Sand Bars are almost entirely confined to the south-
eastern coast-line. The Loo Bar consists of coarse sand and fine
quartz gravel, with occasional pebbles of slate and flint. In 1837 [4]
a boring was made in the middle of the Loo Bar to a depth of 68
feet, or 30 feet below low-water, without meeting rock. The details
of the boring are not given. The waters of the Loo Pool, at a
point 400 yards within the bar, are 40 feet in depth at their ordinary
level. [5]

Swan Pool is dammed by a bar, chiefly composed of small quartz
pebble shingle, 80 yards in breadth, and from 3 to 5 feet above high-
water mark on its crest.

At the mouth of the Pentuan Valley a bank of coarse granitic
sand, in alternate light and dark (schorlaceous) layers, showing false
bedding, and rising to a height of 5 feet above high-water mark,
separates the alluvial land (also superficially composed of granitic
sand) from the sea. A second ridge is formed by a low range of
sand dunes at 6 chains inland, probably the sun-dried drift from the
bank which dams the sea from the low-lying land at the mouth of
the valley.

A low range of sand dunes runs across the head of the Par
Estuary, separating the alluvium from the sea-sands. Par Sands,
being of considerable extent, and uncovered for a long time between
the tides, would furnish the material for this Æolian drift.

[1] Trans. Roy. Geol. Soc. Corn. vol. iii. p. 131.
[2] Ibid. vol. ii. p. 136, and vol. iii. p. 131.   [3] Ibid. vol. vii. p. 31.
[4] Mr. J. Rogers, ibid. vol. vii. p. 352.   [5] Ibid.

PART II.

A CLASSIFICATION OF THE PLEISTOCENE DEPOSITS OF CORNWALL.

OLDEST DEPOSITS.

The existence of a quartz gravel in a district composed of Diallage and Serpentine on Crousa Down, and the occurrence of a similar gravel resting on granite in Crowan, both patches being not only disconnected with the present drainage system, but situated at such altitudes as to preclude the idea of transport from adjacent sources, lead one to infer :

1st. That (a) they were formed from the degradation of the Killas and its associated quartz veins; or (b) from the disintegration and transport of a quartz conglomerate rock.

2nd. That they are the relics of deposits originally much more extensive, formed at a time when the country possessed an entirely different configuration.[1]

There being no means of arriving at a definite conclusion as to the age of these gravels, or of the sands and clays of St. Agnes Beacon, I can only include them within a long period ranging from Cretaceous to early Pleistocene times, at the same time inclining to the belief that the quartz gravels are either of Tertiary age or a re-assortment of Tertiary gravels.

This indefinite chronology is not to be wondered at, when we reflect on the absence of evidence respecting the extension of Cretaceous and Tertiary deposits to the westward of Haldon ; and speculate, in the event of such extension of either formation having taken place, on the influence local sources of supply would have had on the marginal sediments there thrown down.

[1] This is also Mr. Tyack's opinion.

The small flint and quartz pebbles noticed in soil on the top of the cliffs near Trewavas Head, might likewise be considered as of Tertiary origin.

Mr. A. Smith [1] mentions the occurrence of small chalk flints not much worn, and of fragmentary stones of Greensand on the surface of Castle Down, on the north part of Tresco Island.

Mr. Peach [2] speaks of the "Chalk of No Rest" off the Dodman Point. Both these observations require confirmation, especially the latter, so I give them without further comment.

The sands and clays of St. Agnes, occurring at a height of from 350 to 400 feet above the sea, and occupying a site quite disconnected with the present drainage system, carry us back to a time so far removed from the present, that subsequent agencies have obliterated the relations of their site to its original surroundings, in the elaboration of a new drainage system. If, as De la Beche suggested, they are of marine origin, deposited, as Messrs. Kitto and Davies think, in "a sheltered arm of the sea, into which a river emptied its waters," the land must have been submerged to a depth of 400 feet, and therefore their origin must be put back to a time very much more remote than that during which the Raised Beaches were formed.

The exceptional development of clay where the deposit rests on granite, and the peculiarly local character of the pebbles and boulders met with in the different pits, seems to me to forbid a marine origin. The thinning out of the clay toward the edges of the main deposit, as shown in Section F and Pit No. 2, and in Section B in Messrs. Kitto and Davies's paper; the impersistent character of the beds, as shown in the three sections of Pit No. 1; the absence of all organic remains, save a very doubtful plant-like marking, are much more easily explainable by fluviatile than marine action. The exposure in 1875 of a cliff face (part of which is shown in Section F) 16 feet high, at 15 feet from the surface, with very large pebbles, boulders, and angular fragments near its base, corroborates the information De la Beche obtained, and might be taken as proving marine action; but, on the other hand, the very great irregularity in the shelf in some stream-tin sections, the existence of false shelf

---

[1] Trans. Roy. Geol. Soc. Corn. vol. vii. p. 343.

[2] *Ibid.* vol. v. p. 55.

in some places, and of large masses of slate in the gravels (from the disintegration and fall of rugosities in the river-bed or banks) in others, renders it possible that the water-worn face and outstanding pinnacle of the cliff may be due to fluviatile agencies.

The preservation of the sands and clays is probably due to an envelope of talus shed from time to time through the weathering of the high land of the Beacon (620 feet above the sea), and represented by the overburden or Head in the sections. This Head was, in all probability, accumulated after a considerable denudation of the deposits had taken place, so that it rested directly on the sands on the edges of the patch. Such appearances as the inosculation of the Head with the upper bed of sand in pit No. 3 might be explained by rain floods carrying *débris* over an eroded surface of sand, and by the penetration of winter frosts, causing the intrusion of the earthy material in the hollows of the surface on which it rested. I see no reason to doubt the contemporaneity of the overburden with the Head on the cliff-line.

The local character of the pebbles in the deposit might be considered as an objection to the fluviatile theory. I assume, however, the former existence of a stream draining districts of similar constitution to the present surroundings of the patch, and account for the variety of the sediments not only by fluctuations in the condition of the stream, but by its conversion into a tarn through the stopping of its seaward outlet. The varied alternations of sand and clay would then result from the deposition of a stream, whose finer sediments would be precipitated in the deeper parts of the lake, their precipitation being interrupted by influxes of coarser material when the stream was swollen or the dam temporarily removed.

Their isolation prevents one from assuming that the formation of the sands and clays of St. Agnes was contemporary with the deposition of the Crousa Down and Crowan gravels, but in the absence of connecting links, they may be classed together within a period ranging from Tertiary to early Pleistocene times, when the contour presented a vastly different aspect from its present outlines, before the selection of the present lines of drainage.

BOULDER GRAVELS.

As in the granitic districts of the Land's End, the modern beaches are often almost entirely composed of large rounded granite boulders, it is not improbable that many of the boulder gravels alluded to by Messrs. Carne and Henwood; at Pornanvon, St. Loy, and St. Just, for instance; may represent raised beaches or contemporaneous fluviatile deposits, whilst others in valley bottoms of the present lines of drainage may be equivalent to stanniferous gravels elsewhere. But boulder gravels, such as those mentioned by Mr. Henwood as occurring at a height of 80 feet above the sea at Morrab Place, Penzance, or even the boulder-bed forming the roof of Gamper Hole, at 40 feet above the sea, mentioned by Mr. Carne, cannot be classified with the Raised Beaches, even on the supposition of unequal elevation, as well as a local rise of tide : and still less can they be regarded as equivalent to stanniferous gravels.

It is very difficult to believe that no traces of old fluviatile deposition, prior to the formation of the old beach cliffs (*i.e.* before and during the subsidence which culminated in the formation of the Raised Beaches), were preserved. Before and during the elaboration of the present drainage system, deposits would no doubt have been formed marking the progress of denudation by the rivers. Whilst in inland districts the great surface waste during the period of the accumulation of the Head on the coasts would have tended to the dispersion and concealment of such old fluviatile relics on the slopes, mining excavations, and the wearing back of the coast-line would naturally bring them to light. The boulders at Huel Carn Mine, 50 feet from the surface and 500 feet above the sea, mentioned by Mr. Carne as occurring beneath a mass of disintegrated granite and clay, are probably explainable in this way. The boulders of granite in Rosewarne Mine, Gwinear, at 74 fathoms from the surface, noticed by Mr. Salmon who considered that they had been introduced by fissures from the surface, are so difficult of explanation without further particulars, especially the description of the structure of the granite in their vicinity, that I hesitate to hazard a conjecture respecting them. At Relistian Mine, on the contrary, though the slate pebbles observed by Mr. Carne were met with at 100 fathoms from the surface, his mention of spheroidal concretions in the slate in their vicinity seems to offer at once the simplest and most reasonable explanation. Numerous localities in the Land's End District, in which boulders occur, have been cited by Mr. Carne in Trans. Roy. Geol. Soc. Corn. vol. iii. It is to be regretted that the absence of similar notices of the old gravels in the central and eastern part of Cornwall renders this part of the subject so defective.

When we reconstruct, in imagination, the Cornwall of early Pleistocene times, before the submergence which led to the Raised Beach formation had begun, we can scarcely consider the present extent of the county as embracing more than the main watershed boundary and sources of the old drainage system, so that the paucity of old river gravels is not to be wondered at.

RAISED BEACHES.

From the sections given, the average height of the base of the Raised Beaches may be taken as from 5 to 10 feet above high-water mark ; but, as a considerable thickness of beach has been denuded away from the sites, where traces are only now visible, and as in many places the Head, or talus, was shed upon it while in an uncon-solidated state, partly sweeping away and partly becoming mixed with its sands and pebbles, sections where the whole thickness of beach seems to be present (as in Gerran's Bay, St. Ives, Godrevy Beach, and Fistral Bay) must be taken, which would raise the average extent of subsidence during the Raised Beach formation to 15 feet above high-water mark.

As, no doubt, beaches were in some cases heaped up to a few feet above spring-tide high-water, or were, like the modern West Green Sandbank near Marazion, overspread by the shifting sand grains drifted from the foreshore, the actual thickness of Raised Beaches, where undenuded, is not always a safe index of the amount of sub-sidence.

The height of the old beaches would naturally be greater in proximity to their cliff-line, so that isolated portions, on reefs at the level of spring-tide high-water, or exposed at the base of a consider-able thickness of Head, masking an old cliff some distance inland, are no indices of the local amount of elevation of the beaches.[1]

[1] *Vide* De la Beche, Geological Manual, p. 157 ; and Pengelly, " On Raised Beaches," Trans. Dev. Assoc. for 1866.

The section at Treen Cove, given by Mr. Carne, if an instance of
Raised Beach, is of very exceptional height (20 feet above spring-
tide high-water), and it is not clear whether he regarded the whole
mass, 15 feet thick under the Head, as Raised Beach, or only the
lower part of it.

The paucity of shells in the Raised Beaches, and their very local
occurrence, is worthy of note.[1]

OLD BLOWN SANDS.

It is not easy to fix a definite junction between Old Blown Sands
and Raised Beaches, where both are similarly bedded and consolidated. In the lower parts of the Old Blown Sands of Fistral Bay
and Godrevy Beach pebbles are sparsely disseminated, sometimes
in impersistent lines, having been probably cast up by storm waves.
In the cliffs of Godrevy, Fistral Bay, Towan Head, New Quay,
Greenway (N. of Padstow), the best examples of Old Blown Sands
are shown, attaining in places to 20 feet in thickness.

In Greenway Cliff, and in parts of Fistral Bay, the Old Blown
Sand projects from the cliff face in hard corrugated laminæ of
siliceous sandstone.

In parts of Godrevy Cliff, and near New Quay Pier, the Old
Blown Sand is consolidated in hard thick beds.

HEAD.

Though from its general appearance the Head might be regarded
merely as an old talus, shed from the adjacent heights upon the
raised platform of the old beaches, in some cases fragments have
been incorporated which could not have been derived by mere
weathering, but were probably carried down by torrential surface
waters or melting snows from higher lands not far off, but not in the
immediate vicinity. Where the Head, for instance, caps cliffs forming the seaward termination of a valley, one might expect to find
fragments in it which had travelled some distance. The appearance
of stratification sometimes exhibited might be satisfactorily explained
by seasonal changes. Thus the disintegration and slip of numerous

[1] When the fragmentary condition of the Raised Beaches is taken into account,
as well as, in many cases, the unfavourable nature of their materials for the preservation of shells, except in a microscopically comminuted state, objections to
unfossiliferous deposits being regarded as Raised Beaches will be shown to be
unfounded.—W. C., Sept. 1879.

fragments of earth and soil, through the wedging of frosts and melting snows, might be temporarily succeeded by a finer talus, containing smaller and fewer stones, during milder seasons.

The frequent cliff-sections, composed of a thick masking film of Head resting, as no modern talus could rest, against a rock-face a few feet from its cliffs, coupled with occasional instances of its isolation from the main cliffs, upon rocky reefs on the foreshore, as at Godrevy and Cape Cornwall, point to a very much greater extension of land during its accumulation.

Next as to its age :

1st. It is more recent than the Raised Beaches, because, as Mr. Carne pointed out, where both are present in the same cliff, it invariably rests upon them. A possible exception may be furnished by the Greenway Cliff section, mentioned in the supplementary paper on Padstow.

2nd. It is older than the commencement of the forest growth, for the following reasons :

(a) The Head evidences a period of great subaerial waste, a more rigid climate; both likely to occur when the old beaches attained their maximum elevation, possibly producing continental conditions. The submerged forests must have flourished on a much more extended, though subsiding, area, and that subsidence must have been going on for some time prior to their growth, as the flora does not indicate any marked change of climate from the present : a greater extent of area is also indicated by the depth of the stream-tin gravels at Par, Pentuan, Carnon, etc., below the sea-level.

(b) The Head rests upon the old plane of marine denudation, whilst the forest ground seems to occupy tracts eroded in its surface, as on Dunbar Sands, near Padstow, etc., so that we may infer that a considerable amount of denudation had taken place posterior to the accumulation of the Head, and prior to the growth of the forests.

(c) The Head is never found resting on traces of submerged forest, as we might expect to find it near the old cliff, had their growth been prior to its accumulation.

(d) The Raised Beaches furnish proofs of elevation, and the

forest growth proves that elevation to have been far greater than might be inferred from their present positions. The stream-tin gravels, submerged forests, and overlying deposits, prove the long continuance of a subsidence bringing about the present relations of sea and land. As, from its nature, the Head is more likely to have been accumulated during elevation, and for some time after the ensuing subsidence commenced, I have no hesitation in regarding it as older than the submerged forests.

STREAM-TIN GRAVELS.

The stream-tin gravels, from their position, were evidently deposited prior to the growth of the forest stratum resting upon them, and long before the submergence of the forests took place. The depth of the tin ground below high-water mark (about 64 feet in Mr. Henwood's section of Carnon) indicates a much more extended coast-line. There are of course stream-tin gravels of all ages, but those to which I refer are the deposits exposed in the valleys of Par, Pentuan, and the Fal Estuary, etc., and all such inland gravels as can safely be correlated with them. If these stanniferous gravels were deposited prior to the Raised Beach formation, we should expect the following proofs :—

(a) Deposits in the stream-tin valleys at heights corresponding to those of the neighbouring raised beaches. Whereas the old estuarine gravel near the mouth of the Par Estuary, corresponding in height to the raised beach near Spit Point, rests on a slate platform in which the present bed of the estuary has evidently been excavated.

(b) To find traces of marine deposition or of a marine contour on the inland borders of flats like those of Ludgvan, between Marazion and Penzance ; and these we do not find.

(c) That relics of old fluviatile deposits would rest directly on the stream-tin gravels, whereas parts of the old forest-ground rest upon them, and are overlain by fluviatile and marine deposits, still more recent.

(d) That the detritus of stream-tin gravels would be found amongst the materials composing the raised beaches, which is not the case.

Hence I conclude that the stanniferous gravels are more modern than the raised beaches, and not only posterior to them, but separated by a long lapse of time, during which denuding agencies were ceaselessly at work, and great changes took place in the physical geography of Cornwall.

SUBMERGED FORESTS.

The growth of the old forest, the relics of which have been met with all round the Cornish coast, must have extended over a long period of time. The evident connexion of the Mounts Bay Forest with the bed in Marazion Marsh overlying stream-tin, pointed out by Mr. Carne; and the constant presence of a distinct vegetable stratum, or of detritus mixed with vegetable matter, on the tin gravels in most of the principal sections, points to a general correlation of the submerged forests on the coasts with the forest bed in stream-tin sections. Although the forests may have flourished during the deposition of the stanniferous gravels, for purposes of classification it is more convenient to regard them as bridging over the interval between the deposition of the principal stanniferous gravels and the much more modern fluviatile, marine, and estuarine deposits, beneath which they were entombed.

Several observers have cited the occurrence of hazel nuts, in some cases with branches attached, as proof of a sudden autumnal submergence. As the forests flourished on a slightly modified marine contour, which would probably exhibit a series of terraciform features, during a gradual subsidence sudden encroachments of the sea would take place as these plateaux were successively submerged.

The peaty matter so constantly associated with the forest bed, though it might in some cases be explained by the saturation of an old vegetable soil forming round the trees for centuries, would, as a rule, impress one with the idea that the forest tracts were converted into marshes, by the formation of gravel or sand bars damming back the drainage of the valleys, for some time before the sea regained its old cliff bounds.

The general absence of trees in the central and western parts of Cornwall, owing to the prejudicial influences of proximity to the sea, leads me to think that the forests began to flourish, either during

continental conditions, or at a time when the land stood at such an
elevation as to allow of their growth over a considerable tract beyond
the present coast-line, and yet sufficiently far removed from the then
existing coasts to escape their baneful effects. In opposition to this
it might be urged that there is evidence to show that proximity to
a gradually contracting coast-line did not prove fatal to the growth
of woods on the south coast of Cornwall, till a comparatively recent
date.   For in the ancient tradition of St. Michael's Mount being in a
wood, names of animals long since extinct are retained. "We thus
suppose that Caran meant stag; Da, fallow deer; Byk or Kidiorch,
buck; Yorch, roe, etc."[1] But the old cliff-line, at the foot of which
the narrow belt of woodland (whose traces are alone known to us)
was situated, would ward off the inclement breezes from the north
and west, and probably allow of the growth of trees almost as near
the water's edge as they are now growing at Mount Edgecombe near
Plymouth.   The absence of remains of Felidæ or Pachyderms in the
forest bed, the indications of charred matter (as in the stream-tin
sections of Merry Meeting and Carnon), as well as of shaped wood (as
in the sections of Huel Darlington and Pentuan stream works); the
discovery of human skulls at Carnon and Pentuan; and of a human
skeleton near Tarnon Dean (? Tannerdane), at 22 feet below high-
water, if not an anachronism, tend to fix the date of the submergence
of the forests at a time considerably posterior to the existence of the
extinct cave mammalia; and coupled with the tradition given by
Mr. Couch seem to indicate the contemporaneity of the old race of
men with the animals whose bones are found in association with
theirs, inducing one to think that during a thousand years, at least,
before the time of Diodorus, they witnessed the gradual diminution
of their hunting grounds and the destruction of that part of the then
existing forests that lay beyond the limits of our present coasts.

"Under the alluvial deposits, both of Pentuan and Carnon, remains
of deer were found in the forest bed.   Mr. Couch, after a comparison
with specimens from Ireland, identified them with the Irish Elk
(*Megaceros Hibernicus*). In Truro Museum there are specimens of
Strongyloceros spelæus from Pentuan, and of Roebuck (*C. capreolus*),
and *Bos primigenius* from Carnon.

[1] Couch, Trans. Roy. Geol. Soc. Corn. vol. vii. p. 264, etc.

"Bones of Ruminantia, chiefly cervine, are common; numerous specimens have been obtained, amongst other localities, from Whitsand Bay (in East Cornwall); a few to the east of Looe; at Talland; from Polperro Beach; Lantivet Bay (near Fowey); and from Marazion Beach; but principally from Carnon and Pentuan.[1]

"Mr. Couch[2] mentions the discovery of the skeleton of a large deer near an oak (20 feet in length, and of the circumference of a man's waist), at 30 feet from the surface, near Villendreath, in the parish of Sennen; also of pieces of deers' and elks' horns at 20 feet below the surface in Sennen Bay."

Mr. Henwood[3] noticed the respective positions of the human remains found at Carnon and Pentuan.

	Feet below the Surface.	Feet below High-Water Mark.	Feet above or below Low-Water Mark.
At Carnon	58	... 64 ...	46 below.
At Pentuan... ...	20 to 40	... 14 to 34 ...	4 above, and 14 below.

Mr. Couch considered the human skulls unlike those of any of the European races of the present day in their configuration.

In the old river deposits of the valley to the West of St. Austell, remains of *Diatomaceæ* and freshwater shells were found in silt; and in the marine deposits beneath, sea shells, such as *Cardium edule*, of a large size and of a configuration very different from those now inhabiting the same shores.

RECENT MARINE AND FLUVIATILE DEPOSITS.

To particularize the events denoted by the deposits overlying the forest bed in stream-tin sections is unnecessary, as they involve the reiteration of estuarine, turbary, or fluviatile conditions, dependent on the situation of the section with reference to the sea, and the recurrence of local stoppages or diversions of drainage, etc.

Some care is necessary in distinguishing the forest bed proper from the peat beds so often intercalated with more recent estuarine or fluviatile deposits. These peat beds show that a decreased rainfall had brought about the more moderate fluviatile conditions of the

[1] Trans. Roy. Geol. Soc. Corn. vol. vii. pp. 233, 264, etc.   [2] *Ibid*.
[3] Journ. Roy. Instit. Corn. vol. iv.

present time, that morasses had been formed, at different times and in different places, from alterations in river courses or stoppages of drainage, and had in some cases perhaps been temporarily converted into a soil favourable for the growth of underwood, as may be inferred from bed (c) in the Fowey Valley Section.

Mr. Godwin-Austen commented on the occurrence of rock reefs with planed surfaces occupying an intermediate position between high-water mark and the height above it of the neighbouring raised beaches. Numerous examples of such reefs occur, their surfaces ranging from spring-tide high-water to 4 or 5 feet above it; in very many cases they may be regarded as relics of the old beach plane sloping seaward, but in others Mr. Godwin-Austen's idea of a temporary oscillation of a few feet in the later stages of the subsidence which led to the submergence of the forests may be admissible. Such an oscillation would to a great extent explain the formation of such sand and gravel bars as those of the Loo, Swan Pool, Par, and Pentuan; and supposing its cessation and the resumption of the downward movement to have taken place, the destruction of the West Green Sand Banks (near Marazion), and perhaps the entire insulation of St. Michael's Mount, can be readily conceived.

CONCLUSION.

In reviewing the evidence, one cannot avoid being struck with the paucity of Pleistocene deposits in Cornwall, for, notwithstanding their completeness, the stream-tin sections represent but a very small portion of the denudation to which the valleys have been subjected in Post-Tertiary times. Whether we regard the deposits of Crousa Down, Crowan, and St. Agnes as of Tertiary or early Pleistocene age, their positions indicate a configuration vastly different from the present contour, that they were formed at a time when denudation and deposition took place upon tracts of land which have been for ages sparingly acted on by the one, and wholly unmodified by the other.

No direct evidence of glacial action in Cornwall has been obtained. Had the county been invaded by a foreign ice-sheet, or submerged beneath the waters of an Arctic sea, this could not have been the case. Yet, to explain the thoroughness of Pleistocene denudation by agencies sufficiently powerful to sweep away the debris resulting from their erosion, is in a measure to hint at the introduction of ice in some form. There is no reason to think that Cornwall was lower during the period preceding the formation of the old beaches than its present altitude ; but, on the contrary, it is possible that it may have been much higher. Supposing the erosion of the English Channel, as Mr. Godwin-Austen suggests, to have been begun in the early part of the Pleistocene epoch by a river flowing westward, the transport of Cretaceous materials obtained from the eastern districts would have furnished a plentiful supply of flints for incorporation in the subsequent beaches, and their presence both in the raised and modern beaches would be easily accounted for. As the influence of glacial conditions became felt, the highlands would become covered by snow, liberating great quantities of surface-water with torrential power during intermittent warmer periods, and during the succeeding amelioration ; by these causes great surface waste would take place, the valleys would be deepened, and the existing deposits in exposed situations swept down with recently derived materials to lower levels now beneath the sea. The alternative version postulates more than this, namely, the descent of glaciers from the snow-covered highlands. In both cases the observation I have applied to the old boulder gravels holds good, namely, the fact that the present area of Cornwall (at least in its more western parts) would represent but the watershed, or, in the case of ice, the generative sources, and tracks of its nascent flow, and all moraine material, etc., would be swept down to districts now beneath the sea, whilst *roches moutonnées*, etc., would be very unlikely to survive the subsequent extensive weathering of exposed rock surfaces which took place during the accumulation of the Head.

Reasons have been assigned for believing that coast-ice helped to transport some of the materials found in the raised beaches of Brittany.[1] The large granite boulder pointed out by Mr. Williams rests on the old beach platform in Barnstaple Bay, and is surrounded by the raised beach materials which also rest on it. It is evidently an erratic. Some months after my paper on the Pleistocene Deposits

---

[1] Annales de la Soc. Geol. du Nord, T. 4, p. 186, April 18th, 1877.

TABLE OF CLASSIFICATION.

DEPOSITS.	PHYSICAL CHANGES INDICATED.	PERIODS.
12. Sea Beaches, River Gravels, Alluvia and Peat Growth.		The Present
11. Blown Sands.	Gradual overspread of Blown Sands on parts of the North-western coast of Cornwall, entombing hamlets and churches.	Historic. / Post-Glacial.
10. River deposits with estuarine sediments intercalated in some Stream-tin Sections near the coast, also Peat beds. River deposits with occasional Peat beds intercalated in Inland districts.	Local stoppages or diversions of drainage giving rise to peat growth and morasses in valley bottoms. Climate of the Central and Western parts of Cornwall only favourable for the growth of underwood.	
9. Planed Rock reefs, Gravel and Sand Bars.	Possible oscillation in the subsiding movement, not yet counteracted.	
8. Marine and estuarine deposits in some Stream-tin Sections. River Gravels and Alluvia in inland districts.	Advance of the sea to its old cliff bounds; destruction and entombment of the marshy forest lands fringing the coasts; decay of forests in inland districts through the prevalence of unfavourable conditions.	
7. Submerged Forests and Forest Bed in some Stream-tin sections. The presence of man indicated, with remains of deer (including the Irish elk) and oxen.	Continuance of subsidence, gradually circumscribing the forest plains, but allowing sudden encroachments of the sea from time to time as the successive terraces in its old plain were surmounted. Climate ameliorating and becoming suitable for the growth of Oak, Alder, Hazel, etc., on a large area beyond the limits of the present coast-line.	Pre-Historic.
6. Head in inland districts and on the cliffs. River Gravels. Stream-tin Gravels.	Elevation, perhaps culminating in continental conditions. Seasons becoming more marked. Considerable snow-fall and penetrating frosts. Much surface water. Cold diminishing. Subsidence. Rainfall greater than now.	Period of Su aerial wast Correspond ing to the Second Gla cial Period
5. Probably River Gravels, as in Devon, connected with the present drainage system.	Land rising.	Correspond ing to the Intraglacia Period.
4. Raised Beaches and Old Blown Sands.	Culmination of subsidence at an average of 15 feet below the present level: Wales, etc., being submerged, in places, to a depth of 1500 feet.	Glacial Period.
Erratic boulder at Saunton (North Devon).	Stranding of occasional icebergs or floes drifted from Ireland, Lundy Island or the Northern counties.	
3. Boulder Gravels.	Land subsiding. Liberation of much surface water with torrential power by melting of snows during intermittent warm periods and the succeeding amelioration.	
2. Deposits not recognizable. Debris swept to lower levels beyond the existing coast-line.	Land at considerable altitude, possibly continental Approach of cold: great quantities of snow accumulating on the highlands (possibly giving rise to a local glacier system).	
1. Gravels of Crousa Down and Crowan; Sands and Clays of St. Agnes.	Old surface configuration prior to the initiation of the present lines of drainage.	Preglacia

of Devon had been read, I visited the spot, and am inclined to think that the boulder was brought by floating ice. These observations lead me to conclude that Cornwall was at a much greater altitude, but sinking during the Glacial epoch, and that, although partaking in the subsidence which caused the submergence of land to a depth of 1,500 feet in the districts further north, its greater altitude when the subsidence began allowed of the existence of a dry land area till its close, which was marked by the formation of the raised beaches when the land stood at an average of 15 feet below its present level. It was during this last period, when glacial conditions were passing away, that I conceive the granite boulder was floated from districts far to the north, or from Ireland. In the accompanying table of classification I have ventured to insert such hypotheses as the foregoing to bridge over the breaks occasioned by the paucity of early Pleistocene deposits in Cornwall.

NOTES ON THE PLEISTOCENE DEPOSITS

OF THE

CORNISH COAST NEAR PADSTOW.

The quaint little chapel of St. Enodock rises from a hummocky expanse of blown sand flanking the Camel Estuary opposite to Padstow. The broad valley occupied by the sand narrows where it terminates in a low sand bank, to the foot of which the sea comes at high tides; this sand bank forms the centre of a little bay, the horns of which are composed of purplish red and greenish banded slates, forming low cliffs, upon which traces of a raised beach are visible in places. The following sections were taken on the cliffs to the north of the bay.

West of Lower Trebetherick :

Blown sand		
Red brown earth		
Small fragments of slate with pebbles and subangular fragments of quartz	3ft.	0in.
Angular slate fragments		
Brown sand with small quartz and flint pebbles resting on slates at 5ft. above high-water mark	4ft.	0in.

In another place to the west of Trebetherick Point.

Blown sand		
Sand with fragments of *Mytili* and *Patellæ* scattered through it (probably blown)	3ft.	0in.
Consolidated sand...	1ft.	0in.
Reddish-brown earth with small fragments of slate, and angular, subangular, and well-worn quartz stones. A large quartz pebble was noticed at the base	1ft.	0in.
Fine brownish sand with occasional small pieces of slate, angular slate fragments, often large, and a few small quartz pebbles	1 to 3ft.	0in.

Bands of sand and loam occur in this basement bed in an adjacent spot. The base of the deposit is from 5 to 7 feet above high-water mark. Mr. Henwood[1] mentioned the occurrence of a layer of angular stones mixed with a few quartzose pebbles on the south side of Trebetherick Point, at about 10 to 12 feet above the present beach.

The same observer noticed the agglutination of sand forming patches of recent sandstone, which has been used in parts of St. Enodock's Chapel, on the north-west of Brea Hill.[2]

The chief interest in the locality attaches to that part of the Dunbar, or Doombar, sands which is left dry between mean tide level and the sand bank in the centre of the little bay called by Mr. Henwood "Daymer Bay." A small stream trickles through the sand bank near the southern side of the bay. At from 70 to 80 yards from the sand bank, and at about six feet below high-water mark, a crust of yellowish, or buff-coloured, laminated consolidated sand, made up chiefly of comminuted shells, and containing sub-angular fragments of quartz and slate, often of large size, firmly imbedded in it, together with shells of *Mytilus*, *Littorina*, etc., etc., projects in ragged reefs through the modern sand-beach which is strewn with fragments of slate and quartz, probably redistributed relics of the older beach.

In one spot a large quartz boulder (FIG. 1), with its lower part firmly cemented in the laminated sandstone, occupies a basin-shaped depression in the reef, the laminæ having a quaquaversal dip toward

FIG. 1.   DUNBAR SANDS.

Reef of Old Consolidated Beach with Quartz Boulder projecting through the present Sands, also a Bed of Peat (*p.*)

About $\frac{1}{20}$ of the natural size.

[1] Fortieth Ann. Rep. R. Instit Corn. for 1858.   [2] *Op. cit.*

it: thus the ordinary action of the tide in forming hollows under any heavy substances encountered on a sand beach has been fossilized and preserved for ages.

(FIG. 2). On the north side of the streamlet, side by side with the old beach reef, and in places only a few feet from it, I observed a mass of blackish peaty matter containing twigs and land shells in a very fragile condition.

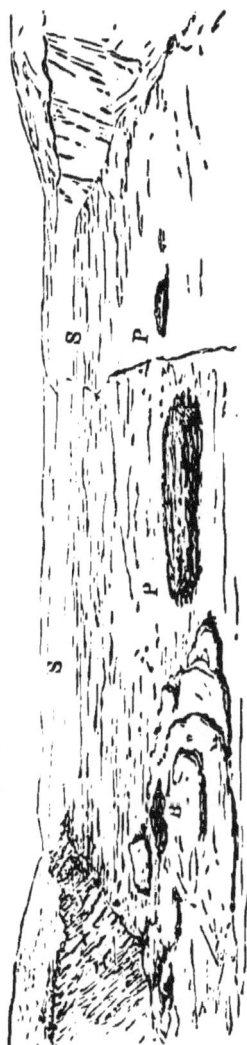

FIG. 2. MOUTH OF THE ST. ENODOCK VALLEY, DUNBAR SANDS.
Showing relative positions of Peat patches and Old Consolidated Beach.

B Old Consolidated Beach. P P Peaty matter. S S Sand Hills.

Mr. Parfitt, of Exeter, kindly identified the few specimens I brought away as *Helix nemoralis* var., *Bythinia tentaculata* and a small *Physa*. The masses of peaty matter were little more than a foot above the surrounding sand when I visited the spot, so that the base of the stratum was nowhere observable. During the 17 years which had elapsed between Mr. Henwood's visit to this spot and my own, considerable changes must have taken place, both in the destruction of the vegetable remains, and in the exposure of the old consolidated beach reefs. Mr. Henwood [1] says that, "In a small bay (called Daymer Bay), between Brea Hill on the south-east and Trebetherick Point on the north-east, a layer of earth, often replaced by clay, and containing fragments of slate and roots of trees *in situ*, protruded through the Doombar sands, traceable on slate rock from above high-water to below ordinary low-water mark, without reaching its boundary in either direction." The roots were found spreading for 20 feet horizontally and erect; they were of oak and hazel, and surrounded by successive layers of leaves and nuts, alternating with thin beds

[1] *Op. cit.*

of sand and earth, in which horns of red deer were found, upon vegetable mould containing shells similar to those now living on the adjoining sand hills.

We have here a true example of a submerged forest, which, coupled with the raised beach on the adjacent cliffs, and the old consolidated beach reef, gives a fair epitome of the later Pleistocene history of Cornwall.

The beach reef is the only example that I know of, in Devon and Cornwall, of an old beach below high-water mark, and this is the only locality in which I have seen old beaches marking different stages in the movement of elevation.

The raised beach indicates a depression of 5 to 10 feet, and a subsequent elevation of more than that amount during a pause in which the beach below high-water was formed, at a time when the relations of sea and land were as at present. But the lower beach must have been also elevated, to allow of its consolidation; and that elevation must have been of such an extent as to favour the growth of forests on the old marine plain, partly shorn of its deposits by subaerial denuding agencies. Finally, a period of subsidence led to the advance of the sea over its old grounds, gaining a plentiful supply of beach materials from the relics of its old deposits, and from river gravels, and causing the decay of the forests and their final entombment in its sands.

GREENWAY CLIFFS.

Proceeding northwards from the Camel Estuary towards Pentire Point, a very interesting section is presented in one part of the coast to the south of Hayle Bay, called Greenway on the Ordnance Map; shown in the diagram on opposite page (FIG. 3).

The cliff face, where uncovered by drift and talus, consists of nearly vertical grey slates, against which, in two places, old consolidated blown sand (A A) abuts, consisting of hard thin beds of calcareous buff-coloured sandstone, dipping seaward at an angle of 20°.

Upon a narrow rocky ledge at the base of the cliff, at about five feet above high-water mark, traces of a raised beach (B B), consisting of coarse consolidated sand, made up of comminuted shells and slaty debris inclosing pebbles, were observed, in one spot, adhering to the slate reef. The base of the old consolidated blown sand rests upon the rocky platform. Near the traces of raised beach the cliff face is composed of brown loam (C), with numerous small angular slate fragments, and occasionally a few large pebbles and blocks of quartz and slate. This stony loam or "Head" is about 15 feet in thickness. It is capped by 4 or 5 feet of gravel (D), consisting of large and small pebbles and angular and subangular fragments of grit, quartz, slate, and greenstone, in grey loamy earth. In one part near its junction with the slates, angular slate fragments predominate in the gravel. The cliff is much obscured by talus concealing the junction of C and D with the slates, in which they appear to occupy an eroded hollow. The base of the gravel (D) is rather more than 20 feet above high-water mark.

FIG. 3. GREENWAY CLIFF.

Vertical Scale—1 inch = 24 feet.

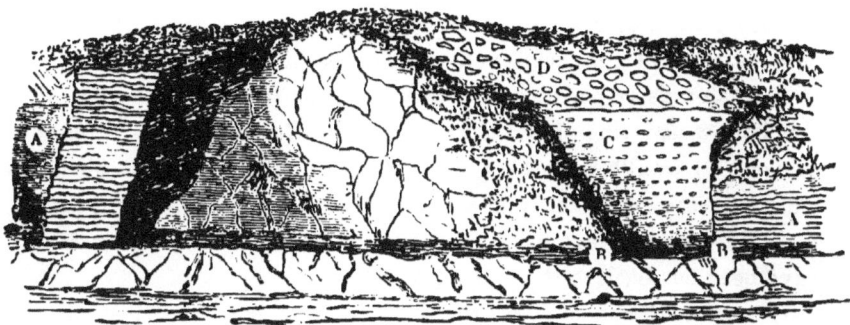

If the gravel D is a raised beach, it must be either older or newer than the old consolidated beach on the reef below. If older, the stony loam (C) would date back to a time anterior to the raised beach formation, and would have been subsequently submerged to allow of a shelf being cut in it, and the deposition of a gravel beach at 20 feet above present high-water mark. The absence of signs of beach at this height in a neighbourhood where the raised beaches seldom exceed 10 feet above high-water mark; the unconsolidated character of the gravel; and the friable nature of the "Head" on which it rests; negative the idea that D is a raised beach of older date than B. Supposing D to be a raised beach of subsequent date to B, then the beach (B) would have been raised, the stony loam (C) precipitated upon it, and a subsidence, for which we have no analogy on any other part of the coast, would have taken place, allowing the deposition of D.

Apart from the negative evidence of analogy, this hypothesis is untenable; for, as the old, now consolidated, blown sands bore the same relations to the raised beaches that are exhibited by present blown sands to the modern beaches, the sand would hardly have had time to consolidate before the supposititious subsidence had brought it within reach of the waves, and, if it had consolidated, one would expect to find some trace of a shelf cut in its projecting mass at a height corresponding to the base of the gravel a few yards distant from it.

The gravel D must be regarded as a fluviatile deposit; but in this case two hypotheses as to its age present themselves. First, let us suppose D to be older than the raised beach. Then the stony loam (C) would first have accumulated, either as an ancient talus or flood gravel, in a channel cut in the slates, at a time when the country stood at a higher level. In process of time, from access to fresh materials (regarding C as fluviatile), or from the selection of this hollow as a line of drainage (regarding C as talus), the boulder gravel (D) would have been deposited, and when the subsidence had progressed sufficiently to allow of the formation of an old beach reef, the previous extension of the fluviatile deposit seaward would have been cut back to the present cliff-line.

Let us next suppose the gravel D to have been deposited since the raised beach formation. Then during the elevation of the beach to a much greater height than its present level, the slow process of agglutination would have been at work upon the existing blown sands, and the old beach plain would have been covered with talus, or "Head," near its cliff margin, the result of meteoric waste. In process of time a stream channel would have been formed in the part of the cliff where the talus (C) had accumulated, and the gravel (D) would have been brought down and deposited on the desertion of its channel by the stream. Between these two hypotheses it is not easy to decide.

Unless the stony loam (C) is regarded as a fluviatile deposit, and not a "Head," or atmospheric talus, its position on either of the foregoing hypotheses furnishes a notable exception to Mr. Carne's conclusion as to the "Head" never being found below either raised beaches or boulder gravels. In other respects the numerous observations I have made on the Cornish coast fully corroborate this conclusion. Regarding C as an old fluviatile deposit, which the tendency to horizontal distribution in its contained fragments might warrant, I should prefer to fix the date of the overlying gravel as anterior to the raised beach formation, in accordance with the first hypothesis.

In conclusion, I have to express my sincere obligations to Dr. Henry Woodward for his kind advice and assistance in correcting the proofs of these papers, and insuring the best means for their publication.

STEPHEN AUSTIN AND SONS, PRINTERS, HERTFORD.

www.ingramcontent.com/pod-product-compliance
Lightning Source LLC
Chambersburg PA
CBHW022030080426
42733CB00007B/785